YOUR JOURNEY TO BECOMING UNSKIPPABLE®

(IN YOUR BUSINESS, LIFE & CAREER)

JIM F. KUKRAL

CONTENTS

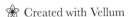 Created with Vellum

INTRODUCTION

$\mathcal{U}$ntil 1954, the world believed that running a four-minute mile was impossible. In the 1940s, the record for running a mile was 4:01 but nobody had even come close to matching or beating that time since. It was commonly believed the human body simply couldn't physically go that fast, and that the body would break down and collapse under the pressure. Everyone said anyone who tried was crazy.

That didn't stop Sir Roger Bannister, who overcame impossibility, all the naysayers and the odds to turn in a time of 3:59.4 on May 6, 1954. But that's not the entire story. Bannister spent years training and sacrificing his body to be a world-record holder.

He earned his way to University at Oxford, and even ran in the 1952 Olympics, in which he disappointedly placed fourth overall. His disappointment was so great that he almost gave up running completely. After a two-month break of thinking about what he wanted to do with his life,

Bannister decided to prove to himself, and everyone else, that he could do better.

So he trained even harder than before, and he trained his way. Slowly but surely he saw himself getting closer to the four-minute mark. He saw that other runners were trying to do the same, including Australian John Landy, his most heated rival. Bannister pushed even harder.

Then came May 6, 1954. All the experts said that "if" the four-minute mark "could" be broken it would be on a day with no wind, and at a certain temperature and only on a specific clay track, and only in front of a massive crowd cheering them on to victory. May 6 was no such day.

The track that day was wet and cold and only about 3,000 people attended. Bannister wasn't sure he was going to run because the conditions were not ideal. He spent the morning working at his day job at the hospital, and he monitored the weather out of his window.

The wind was blowing heavy, and later in the afternoon it began to rain. Not a good day to try and break a record. His rival, Landy, decided to skip the event all together because he believed the conditions made it a waste of his time.

But Bannister didn't skip it. He decided to run anyway.

For the first three laps Bannister kept his normal pace, and by the beginning of the final and fourth lap he had a time of 3.01, meaning he needed to finish the final lap in 59-seconds to break the record.

Bannister was neck and neck with another runner and even lost the edge in the first straightaway. But then he realized this was his chance and overtook all the runners and finished ahead of them all, and with the world record.

He collapsed to the track exhausted and wondered if he had done it. That's when the announcement came over the PA system that he had, in fact, broken the world record and accomplished an under four-minute mark for the mile. His world-record time was 3:59.4.

And just like that, Bannister had become Unskippable.

Here's where the story gets really interesting. Forty-six days after Bannister broke the world record, his rival Landy beat Bannister's time.

Why? Because once you stop believing something is impossible, it becomes possible.

In fact, over the next several years, more and more runners broke the four-minute mark because they too started to believe what was possible. And to date, over 2,000 runners have accomplished this feat as well.

What is impossible to you? Is it that you can live a happy life and live your passion? Because that's already being done. Is it that you want to build a successful business? It's already being done.

Maybe you want to impossibly disrupt your industry like Netflix or Apple has done? Do you think Steve Jobs believed in impossibilities? Maybe you want to have the career you've always dreamed about where you wake up every day excited to go to work?

Again, it's already being done.

You can choose to treat the word impossible as a positive or negative. You can make a conscious decision to believe in it, or overcome it.

You begin the journey to becoming Unskippable in your business, life or career when you start believing that the impossible, is possible.

Let's begin.

66 *"Doctors and scientists said that breaking the four-minute mile was impossible, that one would die in the attempt. Thus, when I got up from the track after collapsing at the finish line, I figured I was dead."*

- Sir Roger Bannister

* * *

*D*ear Reader,

If you've read any of my other books or have seen me speak you know I do things a little bit differently than most. I consider myself an inspirationalist. That's a fancy way of saying I communicate by telling inspiring stories and asking a lot of questions in an attempt to get you thinking, and of course, hopefully taking action.

My goal here is to inspire you to take actions that will help you become Unskippable, whether that's in your business, your life, or in your career.

I love the concept of gold mining. The idea of putting your hands in the dirt and mining for nuggets; even conceptual ones. That's what this book is; a collection of thoughts and stories and case studies (the pay dirt), that contain some valuable and shiny nuggets you will extract then cash in at the gold store.

We'll call them epiphany nuggets. I assure you, they are more valuable than real gold.

Is this a business book? Yeah, sort of. There are certainly a lot of business case studies in the pages to follow, and yes, in the overall scheme of things, we'll be focusing on those business lessons quite a bit. However, what I'm really hoping to do is help you to think much bigger.

You see, there's so much more to life than wealth and making money. I'm pretty sure you get that already; or at least I hope so. Do you really think "bigger picture" when you read typical "business books"?

Look, I've written a bunch of business books. Books for entrepreneurs. Books for authors. Books for marketers and small business owners. This book is like those books in some ways, but deeper, more meaningful.

Let me tell you a story about my own epiphany nugget.

When I first came up with the concept of Unskippable, I found it was the perfect explanation in my head of what I define as a person or business or marketing strategy that is doing something right.

In other words, if you're Unskippable, you're probably pretty successful, and it's the reasons behind why you're successful that fascinate me to no end.

Like you I've always dreamed of doing something bigger, or greater in my life and career. I've set goals for myself and have worked to try and achieve them. I've met a lot of those goals. Here are a few.

1. Own my own business and have no boss. For the past 20 plus years I've accomplished that goal. Check.
2. Have children and raise them to be smart, kind and positive humans who will make the world a better place. Check.
3. Work on what I love and am passionate about. Check.
4. Inspire and teach people how to be happy and live their dreams. Check.
5. Help the Cleveland Browns win the SuperBowl. Sorry, no checkmark here, yet. #crossedfingers

Did you notice that nowhere in that short list is anything about getting rich? Sure, I'd love to be independently wealthy only because in my view money just makes life easier with less worry.

But for me, if having a bunch of money meant I had to sacrifice **ANY** of those things listed above, then forget it, I'm out.

Unfortunately, most of us define success as being wealthy. Society has told us we need to have a fancy car, a big house, and accumulate lots of expensive toys to "make it". We are also told that winners are the people who get rich and the losers are those who don't.

A lot of business books follow this line of thinking. This is why you see so many books about getting rich, and countless gurus and personalities telling you how you can be just like them if you do X, Y & Z and follow their formula.

That's not what this book is about.

Do you want to be rich? Great! Get to work and do it. Is your life goal to accumulate wealth because you think it'll make you happy? More power to you. Is your definition of success to own a multi-billion dollar global brand and have everyone in the world know your name? Wonderful. I hope you do it.

Being Unskippable isn't about being filthy rich.

Being Unskippable isn't about being famous.

Being Unskippable is about mindset, and the specific actions you take to achieve YOUR goals and dreams.

Being Unskippable could mean something as small as being a great parent and raising great kids. Being Unskippable could mean coming up with a great business idea and building a successful business. Being Unskippable could mean getting your dream job by working hard and trying your best.

It's a mindset for your personal viewpoint of success and happiness. Because some of you value money as the pinnacle of success, and some of you (like me) don't even have it in the top 10 of your list.

Whichever way you view money and wealth, for the purpose of this book, it doesn't matter. Because this book is meant to inspire you to be Unskippable in your own unique way.

There are two types of people in the world.

#1 - Skippable people and businesses

#2 - Unskippable people and businesses

Here are some observations to give you more of a feel of where this book will take you.

Skippable people are negative, blame others, are selfish and, in general, are people that are not pleasant to be around.

Unskippable people radiate positivity, accept their own faults, give till it hurts and in general are people everyone wants to be around.

Skippable businesses care about making money at all costs at the expense of their customers.

Unskippable businesses put their customers first and focus on providing massive value above profits.

Skippable people are afraid of failure, and certainly don't innovate or take risks.

Unskippable people fail until it hurts, and certainly try to disrupt and innovate.

Skippable businesses don't stand for anything, and they absolutely don't care what their customers believe in.

Unskippable businesses understand their customers' beliefs and absolutely try to share those beliefs with them.

Skippable people spend their entire lives unhappy and feeling unfulfilled.

Unskippable people reject the belief that they have to be unhappy, and they choose to fill their lives with fulfilling and rewarding experiences.

Pop quiz. Which one do you want to be?

I'm so tired of how we idolize rich, successful people and their accomplishments. Amazon is certainly an Unskippable business, but is its founder Jeff Bezos some kind of God? Not even close. Bezos built a company we buy stuff from; he didn't cure cancer. Let's get some perspective.

An Unskippable person is a hospice nurse who spends their life dedicated to providing care to people who are dying.

An Unskippable person is a friend who is there for you in your darkest hour.

An Unskippable person is the person who walked past you in on your lunch break on your worst day ever and offered a smile.

An Unskippable person is someone who gives their time, energy and money to people less fortunate without asking for kudos.

What is it that you want from your short life? Is it to only be known as a successful business person, or is there something more? So, while most of this book is about business lessons, I would like you to also consider how you can apply these lessons to your life as well.

Because we're only here for a blink of an eye, and the smallest of gestures or actions can make you Unskippable in someone else's life.

Two days after my father's funeral I was drawn to his

favorite drug store where he used to go every Sunday to get the newspaper for the coupons. I didn't shop at this store regularly like my father, but that morning as I was driving by I decided to pull in.

As I was walking around the store an older gentleman walked up to me and grabbed my arm with a smile, and proceeded to tell me silly jokes for ten minutes, which I loved. He was about my father's age, and he told corny jokes like my father had. Eventually the man's wife found him telling jokes to me and pulled him away.

That man made himself Unskippable to me, and he had no idea how much he meant to me. I'll remember him for the rest of my life before I'll ever remember who started Uber or who's at the top of the world's richest person list.

What I am trying to explain is that being Unskippable can sometimes come in the smallest actions and experiences of your life. I want you to fully understand that every little positive, kind and helpful action you take can mean the world to someone else, and possibly change their life forever.

Isn't that what life is really all about?

I've been writing this book in my head for years, and when I finally sat down to put it to paper, it came at a very difficult time. You see, I have a wonderful life and comfortable business. I have great kids, a wonderful wife, a nice home and we are all healthy. I'm blessed and I know it. I can't complain.

However, the past few years have been some of the most difficult years of my life. You'll hear why later on in this book. For now, just understand this: What I went through felt like being put through a meat grinder, then spit out onto the pavement and then run over by a garbage truck. It almost ruined me professionally, financially and spiritually.

Like you, I've also felt, at times, that my life and career didn't measure up to society's standards. Why? Because I put myself up against impossible standards of "success". It wasn't until I reached my late forties that I was able to get over those feelings of inadequacy and instead focus on what I've done right, and what my version of being Unskippable means to me.

I want to be transparent with you. Some of you read the above admission and may have wondered why I would ever reveal these feelings of inadequacy. Let me explain. I don't want you to read this book and think I'm some millionaire or self-help guru that has all the answers.

I'm not, by far. In fact, I'm probably just like you - a person who struggles to provide for their family and has just as many mental, physical and financial problems as everyone else.

Too many books are written by people who want to tell you how successful they are in business and life. Most of us are more than eager to listen to those people because "hey, they've done it, and I want to be like them." I get it.

This book wasn't written to impress you. It's intended to inspire you. Because really, the most impressive thing about me is my family and success of running my own business.

My point is that I'm nobody in society's ultra narcissistic view of success. I don't own a Ferrari. I don't have a second home in Hawaii. I don't go clubbing and spend thousands on bottle service in fancy nightclubs.

Chances are you aren't that person either.

I'm a teacher at heart. I love helping people think differently, and inspiring them to get better and succeed. I have not "made it" in terms of financial wealth. I could not retire today, and wouldn't even if I could.

I'm just a regular guy, making his way the only way I know how.

I wrote this book for you, because I am you. I hope you enjoy it and it inspires you to become Unskippable in your own way, whether it be your business, your life, or your career. Or all of them!

* * *

What Makes Me Unskippable?

I get asked this a lot. Here's my answer (my version of success).

I'm Unskippable because I have raised two wonderful, kind and amazing children who are going to make the world a better place and brighten people's lives through their actions.

I'm Unskippable because I have a 100 percent attendance record at all of my children's sporting events, choir concerts, plays, parent-teacher conferences and family dinner time.

I'm Unskippable because I haven't had a job working for someone else in almost two decades. Instead, I have been able to provide for my family through my own hard work and businesses I have built. I am not rich, but I make enough money to have a comfortable life doing what I love to do.

I'm Unskippable because I wake up every day excited to go to work and help people.

Unfortunately, most people who ask me this question are really asking me "how successful are you in business and how rich are you?" But that's the wrong question to ask someone like me, because I don't define success as financial wealth or how many employees I have.

I define success as all the things I mentioned above. I'm Unskippable on the terms I have set for myself, and I'm fine with that, and you should be too, on your own terms.

Being Unskippable is an attitude, a perspective, an outlook. It's your definition of success; not someone else's. You can spend your entire life trying to live up to what other people have told you successful is, or you can stop, take a breath, and make your own definition, then shoot for that. Chasing someone else's dream usually doesn't work out. I know, I've tried it and have failed miserably.

You need to ask yourself what makes YOU Unskippable, and then go and get it. Life is short.

Have you heard of the Boston Stapler company?

No? How about Swingline staplers? "Yup, that's the one in the movie Office Space. The red one!"

Here's a little bit of trivia if you're a huge fan of the movie as I am. Did you know that Mike Judge, the film's creator, first went to the Boston Stapler company to ask if he could use its stapler in the movie?

First off, out of all the stapler brands, you have to wonder how Judge decided to call them first? It was 1997. Perhaps he just searched for "staplers"? Let's be honest, does the average person really know the brand names of staplers? Of course not. Well, they do now.

But to Judge's surprise, the Boston Stapler company said no to allowing its stapler to be used as a prop in the movie. Maybe they thought it would be making fun of them since it was a comedy? Perhaps they thought "we're a serious, professional brand and we can't be part of a spoof"? Who knows.

But one thing is for sure, saying no was a HUGE mistake.

After the Boston Stapler company said no, Judge went to Swingline and asked if he could use its stapler. They agreed. But there was one catch: Judge wanted a bright-colored stapler that could better be seen on film and Swingline didn't have a red stapler. So, Judge took the existing black Swingline staplers and had them painted bright red.

If you haven't seen the movie, there's an entire plot line of a character (Milton) who's red Swingline stapler is constantly stolen off his desk. It's hilarious.

When the movie comes out, it flops in the theaters only doing about $12 million. But a few years later Comedy Central buys the rights to Office Space. It's aired over and over and suddenly it becomes a huge cult hit. Almost immediately, viewers actually began looking to purchase the red Swingline stapler that they saw in the movie.

But Swingline didn't have such a stapler, so a massive market for replicas grew on eBay where entrepreneurs were making a killing painting staplers red and reselling them.

Picture someone sitting in their basement hand-painting hundreds of black Swingline staplers bright red and then putting them on eBay and making a lot of money. I love entrepreneurs!

Years later, Swingline, seeing that such a huge market for the red stapler exists, decided to produce one themselves. Eureka! In 2002, the Rio Red 747 model stapler was born.

It would become the company's biggest selling stapler and, as the *Wall Street Journal* wrote, "it completely transformed the image of the company".

This all happened because of some free product placement for a product that didn't even exist. In fact, if you go to the Swingline website today, that stapler is still their most prominently featured product, and remains their biggest-seller.

And just like that, Swingline became Unskippable.

Typically there are only a few transformative moments that define success and the difference from being just like everyone else, or making yourself or your business truly known and different. In other words, Unskippable.

In Swingline's example, all it took was a simple "yes" and then capitalizing on demand that appeared out of thin air. Of course, Swingline, I'm sure, never imagined that movie would put them on the map and create a massive, viral outpouring of supply and demand. I mean, they didn't even produce a red stapler.

Let's stop for a second and switch gears and start thinking about your brand. Chances are, you're not as boring as a stapler company. But maybe you are? And that's fine. But it doesn't mean you can't do something about it.

What makes you Unskippable? Do you produce apps? Or maybe you make financial software? Or you're a real estate agent in Montana. Doesn't matter who you are or what you do.

What is Unskippable about your business?

Can't answer that? Keep reading.

Imagine you're in a big room, and you and your competitors are all standing at tables next to each other. In walks a targeted customer there to make a decision between all of you.

Will they choose you? Why do they choose you?

Forget what you've been taught about marketing.

Forget the "I'm cheaper" argument.

Forget the "I'm faster" argument.

Forget the "we have free shipping" argument.

Forget all that stuff.

Yes, those traditional benefit-based marketing strategies still work, and are still important. But those things don't make you Unskippable. Customers don't make decisions on who they are loyal to based upon those factors anymore.

They expect those things.

Ever been to Nebraska? I have not, and I'm sure it's a fine place. But let's face it, if you're the state tourism board tasked with getting people to book a ticket and spend their hard-earned vacation dollars in Nebraska, you've got a tough task ahead of you.

In fact, according to the travel marketing research firm MMGY Global, Nebraska is the state Americans are least interested in visiting. Why? The problem is obvious. There is simply nothing Unskippable about Nebraska.

There's no Grand Canyon. There's no beautiful shoreline of beaches. There's no mountain to climb or amazing national monument to visit. You know what I think of when I hear Nebraska? Corn.

Is that a totally unfair and lame thing to say about what is probably an amazing state? Absolutely it is. But it's the truth and I know I'm not alone on this one.

Selling Nebraska to people who don't live in Nebraska is tough, no doubt. To fix this issue, Nebraska's Tourism Commission hired a branding firm and for $450,000.00 they came up with this pitch: "Nebraska - Honestly, it's not for everyone."

Ouch. Taxpayers spent almost a half-million dollars on that? Yes, they did.

Here's the part where you think I'm going to tell you that it was a huge success, and that Nebraska tourism rates skyrocketed and it was one of the biggest marketing success stories ever. But I can't do that. It failed, miserably.

First of all, you don't become Unskippable by writing a clever tag line. That being said, there is absolutely nothing beneficial or different in the line "Honestly, it's not for everyone."

A better line would probably be, "Nebraska, The Freshest Corn In The World" or "Nebraska, We've Got Corn Out The Ying-Yang. Come Eat Some."

Those lines are totally absurd. But at least they get you thinking or possibly laughing. Even if Nebraska used those instead, you're still not going there and neither am I (and probably never will after the Governor of Nebraska reads this and puts me on the banned list).

Back to the point. Becoming Unskippable is way more than a clever tag line, or logo, or coupon. Those are marketing tactics and strategies.

Unskippable companies transcend their competition.

Unskippable companies are remembered.

Unskippable companies purposely attract loyal customers.

Unskippable companies spend less on advertising because their customers do it for them.

Unskippable companies share common beliefs with their customers.

We'll get to more of that later.

So what in the world is Nebraska going to do to pull themselves out of the depths of being the least visited State in the country? I don't have the answer for that. If I did, I'd be sending an invoice for $450,000 to the Nebraska State Tourism board.

This might be where you are right now with your business or brand or your career or your marriage. You might be Nebraska, and nobody wants to be Nebraska.

You want to be Swingline instead.

I wrote this book for you, all the businesses and brands and regular people that are skippable, to inspire you to become Unskippable. Hopefully, by the end of reading this book you will have a clear understanding of what it takes to truly change how your current and potential customers think about you. Then you will emerge from your cocoon as a beautiful Unskippable butterfly.

Thanks for reading. If you'd like to have a chat with me about ideas for becoming Unskippable, or if you would like to hire me to come speak or do a workshop at your event, please visit www.JimKukral.com.

PART I: THE WORLD HAS BECOME SKIPPABLE

> "Advertising is the tax you pay for being unremarkable." - Robert Stephens, Founder of the Geek Squad.

Take a look around you. Are you riding on a bus? Or sitting in a waiting room? Maybe you're at a coffee shop? Stop for a second and think about every marketing message you are being bombarded with. Every single second of every single moment of your life.

Ugh. The marketing messages are everywhere, even inside video games and pizza boxes, and it's not going away anytime soon. This is nothing new. We're used to the ads and marketing. But that doesn't mean we aren't annoyed by them.

This has been true for a long time. Steve Krug wrote the book *Don't Make Me Think* where he said, "People don't read, they scan."

Absolutely true! Although the book was written in 2000, back when the Internet was still fresh and shiny with a new car smell, it still applies now, more than ever.

You're not "reading" when you quickly scroll through your Facebook timeline on your phone at the red light; you're scanning. You're not "reading" the article about the latest political nonsense; you're scanning it.

Ever post something on social media with all the details in the post (like an event or something), yet then the first comment is a question about the event that was already, clearly, identified in your post?

Yep, because people don't read!

That's the bad news. People are more distracted and rushed than ever and things aren't going to get better. I should know, I wrote an entire book on this topic called "Attention" back in 2010. The same rules we had back then; we have now.

You would have thought things would get better, but they didn't. They got worse.

Our attention spans are not decreasing, we're just getting really good at skipping the stuff that doesn't matter to us.

People pay attention to what interests them, period. We've just become extremely selective of the content we give our limited time to.

This is how binge watching works. You get hooked into some Netflix show you find interesting, then you don't want to stop consuming it, so you watch the entire thing in a few days, or in one sitting. Then you feel disappointed and deflated when it ends.

In other words, we will only spend seconds figuring out what we like and want to pay attention to, but we'll spend much longer with that content once we figure out we like it.

Being Unskippable is when you create moments, stories, products and services that interest a specific person (a targeted customer) so much that they can't stop consuming, and when they do, they're sad and they want more!

We've got a lot of choices in our lives. I mean, a LOT! And most of your choices are right at your fingertips. Pick up the little computer that's in your pocket and ask it for help or a recommendation. You'll get a plethora of choices. That's pretty amazing, isn't it?

"Hey, Siri. Who delivers pizza around me now?"

"Alexa, find me someone to plow the snow off my driveway."

"Hey, Google. Find a coffee shop near me."

As I mentioned, choices are good. Options empower the consumer and keep prices down and quality up. But, with all the choices comes the major dilemma of what or who do you choose?

During the gold rush in the late 1800's, businesses that sold mining supplies in the Yukon became Unskippable because they were the only choice. If you trekked all the way up to the Yukon in search of fortune and forgot your shovel, you're not getting one from the Home Depot. Nope, you're paying 30 times the market value at the only shovel supplier in camp.

But guess what? Chances are you're not the only choice in your industry, so your dreams of becoming Unskippable that way aren't good. It's just not that easy in today's world.

Jay Baer's excellent book *Talk Triggers* famously discusses how The Cheesecake Factory menu is purposely designed to have a ton of choices because, wait for it, because that's what keeps people talking about them. "Did you see the menu at The Cheesecake Factory? There's so many items to choose from!"

Here's the thing. Because we're bombarded with so many ads and choices, our brains have to figure out how to decide.

Typically, businesses rely on traditional benefit-based marketing strategies to help us make up our minds. You know, things like "free shipping" and "coupons" and "fast delivery".

As I mentioned earlier, that stuff works. It has worked forever and will continue to work. But, for consumers, we are now at the point where it's just not enough to help us make a decision. We want more.

Welcome to the future where everyone wants to skip everything. No, not like skipping down the street. I'm talking about buying a car online and having it delivered to your house so you can skip the pushy and inconvenient car dealership. Or skipping the drive-thru line at your favorite fast-food restaurant by ordering on your phone and having it brought out to your car on demand.

The world has become skippable.

DVRs enable us to fast forward through the commercials. When we're forced to watch commercials during live events we have two things on our minds. First, maybe to run to the bathroom. Second, to check our phones.

Sometimes we do both at the same time. Admit it. You know you do it.

In fact, according to CBSNews.com, 75 percent of Americans admit to using their mobile phones while in the bathroom. It's a problem. The report also states that 19 percent of people have dropped the phone in the toilet. Ewww.

When you're watching a show on Netflix they let you skip to the next episode immediately so you don't have to wait those painfully long five seconds for it to start on its own.

We love skipping. The only thing we haven't invented yet is the skip button on a person we dislike. You know someone, somewhere must be working on this. You're at a work party, and Susie from purchasing walks up to you and you're thinking in your head, "I wish I could hit the skip button right now."

We spend an average of over three hours a day looking at our phones. Not talking on them. Looking at them.

The Wall Street Journal reported that, "Teens are spending more than one-third of their days using media such as online video or music — nearly nine hours on average."

But it's not just teens; we all do it. Here's a challenge for you. Grab your phone and check your screen time. If you have an iPhone it's easy. Just go to Settings, then Screen time. I'm at 2 hours and 19 minutes today, and it's only 2:51 pm!

Time Magazine reported on a study saying the average attention span of a goldfish was 10-seconds, and that humans were less than that. The entire thing sounds absurd. In fact, it was completely debunked as false. Go figure, right?

I'm not sure how you would measure the attention span of a goldfish anyway. Then again, as humans we tend to believe things we agree with more than things that we do not. And when somebody like Time Magazine tells us a goldfish can hold a memory at all, we believe it.

The point is, as absurd as it sounds, it also makes sense; we have a lot of distractions thrown at us and technology isn't helping.

A study by Microsoft said that 77 percent of people stated, "When nothing is occupying my attention, the first thing I do is pick up my phone."

I dropped my phone down the steps last week and it shattered into a million pieces. I took it to the Apple store and had to wait two hours for them to fix it. Two whole hours! Talk about a freeing experience.

During those two hours I went to the bookstore, had a coffee and read. I sat down at the patio of a restaurant, people watched and had a conversation with the person at the table next to me.

You know what else I did? I subconsciously kept reaching into my left pocket where I keep my phone, over and over. I did it when I got on the escalator in the bookstore. But there was no phone so I enjoyed the view instead of checking Facebook.

I did it after the waiter took my order, but there was no phone in my pocket. I was completely undistracted from what seemed like everything in the world, and man, it felt great. But reaching for the phone is still a hard habit to break.

My teenagers watch YouTube more than TV, by far. Their modern day commercials are the short video ads that they must pay attention to for a few seconds before they can hit skip.

My son once wanted to show me a video on his phone and as soon as the ad started he's says "Forget it, these ads are horrible. I'm not waiting through this." Then I turn into my father and I give him the dad look. "It's five seconds, son. You can't wait five seconds?"

Apparently, no, he can't. But the reality is he does it all day long.

Gary Vaynerchuk, Chairman of VaynerX, gave a talk to the staffers and executives at Facebook in early 2019 where he spoke about the state of advertising on Madison Ave. He said, "I don't think there's a single human being on Earth that really watches a television commercial." Hyperbole, yes. But, still, he's right - unless it's the SuperBowl.

Companies trying to get attention only have seconds. Think about that. We are all being trained to pay attention for just a few seconds. It's simply not enough time to get a meaningful benefit across. Not really, anyway.

Traditional benefit-based marketing tactics are still the gold standard in marketing. You have a product or a service that solves a problem, and you show the benefit of how you overcome the problem. Pretty easy formula.

But it's just not enough any longer. We have to find ways to become Unskippable.

Did you know that Generation Z (those born between the mid-1990s and mid-2000s) likes to watch "TV" with closed captioning on? It's true. The reason - they say it helps them focus. Now if you're like me, you can sit and consume media without losing focus. But Gen Z? They aren't just watching a show.

In fact, according to Hootsuite, 84 percent of smartphone tablet owners use their devices as a second screen while they watch TV. That number isn't just young people either. It's all of us. Tell me you didn't pick up your phone or tablet just once when you were watching a two-hour American Idol episode.

You can't, because you did.

We want to focus on things we are into, but sometimes we need a little help. Audible, Amazon's audiobook brand, has recently launched a new feature called *Audible Captions* that lets you read along with your audiobook. Why? According to Audible founder and CEO Don Katz, "We know from years and years of work, that parents and educators, in particular, understand that an audio experience of well-composed words is really important in developing learners."

This is all based on something called Immersion Reading. According to Audible, "Immersion Reading takes you deeper into a story than ever before! This functionality allows you to read a Kindle eBook and listen to its professionally narrated Audible companion Audiobook – all at the same time. Not only that, but you get the benefit of real-time highlighting, making Immersion Reading a valuable tool to boost reading comprehension and overall retention of content."

Do you have kids? Like I said, I have a 17 and 14-year-old (at the time of this writing). We try to watch "TV" together as a family every night. Usually, it's an hour-long show where we're all together just hanging out.

So, we put the show *Friends* on and we're all watching. Ten minutes into the show I look over at my kids and they're staring at their phones. That's when I pause the show, and very annoyed I say, "You're not even watching."

Their eyes roll. "We are watching. We're just doing other things too."

Me: "Like what? You are either watching or you're not."

Them: "Dad, just because I'm not staring at the TV doesn't mean I'm not watching."

Me: "Yes, it does, actually."

Them: "Okay, I don't want to argue." (They put their phones down.)

Five minutes later I look up and they're back to looking at their phones and I give up. They're good kids so it's difficult to be hard on them. I'm such a pushover.

I needed to know what they were doing. I forced my daughter (through threat of changing the Wi-Fi password) to let me watch her over her shoulder.

Here's what she was doing while watching *Friends*. Texting with several people. One looked like a large group text string where they were discussing the *Friends* episode that they were all watching together at the same time.

In between text messages, my daughter was also checking Instagram and Snapchat. This meant leaving comments and likes on posts, and actually taking a photo of the TV screen with *Friends* on and posting "My favorite episode of *Friends* is on. The one where Phoebe runs in the park."

Then someone in the text string shares a gif of a funny moment on *Friends* (Monica gets a giant turkey stuck on her head). Then someone shares a YouTube link to another *Friends* meme.

At that point things go off the rails because YouTube is opened and she's now watching a video of some kids who break into abandoned homes and look for treasure, which has nothing to do with *Friends*. Note: She accomplishes this by having one earbud in for the YouTube video, and the other ear open to the show on the television.

That's where she lost me. At least the other stuff she was doing was *Friends* related. I get it. You're having conversations with friends about *Friends*, while watching *Friends*.

I do this all the time with college buddies as we text each other during sporting events we're all watching in different parts of the world. But I'm not watching a rerun of The Godfather while also looking up Godfather memes or listening to a Godfather related podcast, all at the same time. I guess that makes me old.

My point is this - as business owners, entrepreneurs and marketers, do you really think you're going to be able to get through to someone who is all over the board like that? You really think that your free shipping offer is going to be the determining final factor to a 25-year-old who can't focus enough to watch a television show on their own so they have to turn closed captioning on?

You know, it's not. It's going to take way more to get and keep attention in the future. The question is, are you ready for it?

Major League Baseball has a big attention problem. The games are too long, both on television and in the ballparks. There isn't enough action and too much downtime between pitches to keep fans' attention.

This is why you see MLB ballparks putting more social aspects like bars and restaurants into the stadiums, along with free Wi-Fi, and cheaper tickets. Because people are bored, and if you go to a game nowadays you'll notice something. People aren't watching the game, they're just looking at their phones.

This doesn't seem to exist with other professional sports leagues. Nobody cares that NFL games are routinely over three hours. NBA fans do not complain about the final two minutes taking a lifetime to finish. But in baseball? It's skippable, because it's a slow moving game and can be boring.

Rob Manfred, MLB Commissioner, noted in 2018 that attendance is down nearly 10 percent from 2017, making it the sixth season in a row of declining attendance. Major League Baseball is frantically considering rule changes, pitch clocks and fan-friendly scheduling to appeal to the distracted consumer.

But speeding up the game is only a bandaid to the real issue, which is that the consumer has changed.

Say what you want about millennials, but they are not cheap. Millennials gladly shell out $12 for a fancy craft beer and drop $13 on fish tacos at the ballpark or otherwise.

But they are not willing to be bored, at all.

Yeah, I know this isn't everyone who watches baseball. And yes, I know, there are still plenty of people who enjoy baseball in its current form. But let's be honest, the writing is on the wall for the future, and that is being driven by the future baseball consumer.

Baseball must learn how to become Unskippable.

And so do you.

I'm pretty sure I'm preaching to the choir here, but it needs to be said. We're living in a mobile world, which is a determining factor for our lack of attention and why we try to skip so much.

A 2015 Bank of America report found that 71 percent of people sleep with or near their phones, and that includes the 13 percent who said they slept with their phones in their beds. Heck, I know people who take their phones into the shower with them, and in the pool when they're doing laps.

The irony of it all is that we don't even use our phones for calls anymore.

U.S. phones were inundated with 26.3 billion robo-calls last year, a 46 percent increase from the 18 billion spam calls placed in 2017. Whoa! But why? The tech to make such calls has become easy (and cheap) to access, so more robo-callers are jumping into the fray.

The consequence of it all? Junk calls are driving people to avoid (skip) answering the phone altogether, with 52 percent of cell phone calls going unanswered, reports MarketWatch.

When was the last time you answered your phone from a number you don't recognize? These little contraptions hooked to our belts or in our purses aren't "telephones", they're little computers that suck our souls out while we're staring at them.

Okay, that was a bit dramatic. The point is we have lost ourselves with these devices and they are a major contrib-utor to our distractions, and of course one of the biggest reasons we can't seem to focus on pretty much anything for too long.

To summarize: We have phones we don't really use as phones, and we also have social media, which distracts us even more. The funny part is we use our phones to access social media. Yet, in a NBC News/*Wall Street Journal* poll a whopping 82 percent believe social media is a big waste of our time. But still, 69 percent of all Americans still use social media once a day or more, mostly on their phones.

It's a vicious skippable circle. But it's also the reality, and the future we all have to deal with.

Michael Lastoria, founder of the &Pizza franchise that is taking the pizza world by storm, got nearly $60 million in funding to model a new kind of restaurant. One of the driving principles of &Pizza's success (besides the "dough bots" that automate the tedious and most dangerous part of making pizza) is a completely text-to-order platform.

Lastoria stated in an Inc.com article, "You can't call an &Pizza. You can't email us. We won't respond." He continued, "That [text] is the way that most people communicate."

And he's right.

* * *

My Big, Fat, Embarrassing Mistake

I made a huge mistake in 2015. It almost cost me my marriage, nearly decimated my finances, destroyed my business, and also came close to ruining my reputation in my community.

The mistake? I ran for public office in the United States of America and won.

Before I decided to run for office my business was at an all-time high of success and profitability. I had spent over 20 years building a brand and creating businesses that were humming along nicely. I was working maybe two to three hours a day while the businesses ran on autopilot and the money rolled in. I had taken my family to Disney World for vacation in the spring three years in a row, with another beach summer vacation as well, every year.

Because of the free time I had I was able to attend every single event involving my children. I'm talking about 100 percent attendance at every parent-teacher meeting, or choir concert, sporting event, etc.

It was a really good time in my life personally, financially and mentally. So, of course, I decided to go and ruin it all by getting into local politics.

By the time my two-year term was up in 2017 I had almost completely destroyed my business from lack of attention and focus. My marriage was on the rocks due to the pressure and vitriol from politically polarized people who constantly attacked me and my family. And my perfect attendance record was broken as I had to spend more and more time attending city council meetings and attending to residents complaints and questions.

Oh, and did I mention I was so mentally broken down I wasn't sleeping well? I was also grinding my teeth and I was eating more poorly than I ever had.

All for what? A $7,000 a year "job" with no benefits. A job that consumed me and had me working more than 40 hours a week.

Dumb move, Jim.

So, what made me do it? Two reasons. First, I cared deeply about my community and I wanted to be the change I wanted to see. I also wanted to show my children that in this life you need to lead, not follow, and that strong, successful people put themselves out there and care about things they believe in, even when there is a difficult task at hand.

My second reason, the narcissistic one, was that as an entrepreneur I was convinced that running for office would be a breeze and my super-awesome marketing skills would shine through and vanquish my opponent.

It did work actually. I won my first election by a landslide against a two-term incumbent with name recognition. Then two years later, I lost to the same person - by 35 votes. Ouch.

Believe me, losing was a Godsend to me. Have you ever owned a boat? It's like that. The best two days for boat owners are the day they buy it, then the day they sell it.

For me, the best two days were when I won my first election, then when I lost.

However, by running a campaign I learned that I needed to be Unskippable to win.

For the first election I hit the streets, on foot, and went door to door for months. I talked to thousands of people in their living rooms and front porches and shared a soda or a coffee with them. I showed them photos of my family and talked about the neighborhood.

This helped me figure out why people vote. It's not because I offered benefit-based solutions (lower taxes, fix their sewers); remember, people expected those things now. It was because they felt comfortable with me, understood my story and my values and who I was.

As I would say goodbye, I would ask the person if I could put a sign in their yard and a lot of them would say yes. So, I'd go into my car and grab a big yard sign and put it in their front yard, then move on to the next house.

The morning of my first election I drove through my neighborhood and saw hundreds of my signs lining the neighboring streets, with my name "KUKRAL" in big, bold letters, and I knew I had become Unskippable, and I knew I was going to win.

My opponent, on the other hand, was convinced that everyone knew his name and that this new Kukral guy who came out of nowhere was never going to be able to beat him. Because of that he didn't campaign as hard. He didn't go to as many doors as I did and he didn't get as many yard signs as I did.

He broke the #1 rule - he didn't make himself Unskippable. That's why he lost, and I won.

That's when things went bad, really bad.

Listen, winning that first election was a huge moment for me, and my ego. I viewed it as the ultimate personal branding experiment. I had taken all the years of my marketing knowledge and used it to sell myself to real people, real "customers". Not faceless users on the Internet.

So, when I won the first election I was feeling pretty, pretty good about myself.

Unfortunately for me, the two years that followed almost destroyed me in all the ways I mentioned previously. There were times when I was elected that I thought I had ruined my life. There were days I wanted to curl up in a ball and just fade away. The attacks on myself and my family were relentless. The lies told about me were disgusting. The sheer dirty politics of it all broke me.

By the time I had to run again (I had a two-year term) I was already checked out. I didn't want to win, which meant I didn't campaign as hard. Looking back on it now, I wanted to lose, and I did - by 35 votes. Because if I lost I knew I might be able to recover my life, my marriage and my business.

I honestly believe I could not have written this book before that experience; the good and bad parts of it.

Now, almost a year and a half later, I'm almost back mentally and in other ways. But it was a hard climb out of that hole. Winning and losing on your own name, your brand, is personal. It's not marketing a steak sauce, because if people don't buy it, well, you just didn't sell steak sauce.

But when people don't vote for you, it's way more personal because they don't freaking like you, and that's a very hard pill to swallow.

At first I thought I could deal with it, and in many ways I did. The problems came when the job started to affect my family members. I'd get a call from my upset wife telling me about how some crazy lady from the neighborhood recognized her and my daughter and starting screaming and cursing at them. All because they were related to me, the evil Ward 3 City Councilman of Seven Hills, OH.

The same lady then called the police on my wife saying my wife was verbally abusing her, which wasn't true. My wife never said one word to her. But the police were dispatched to my home to interrogate my wife, in front of my children. Nothing came of it of course, because it was false. Nevertheless, it was terrible for my wife and for my kids to experience this.

Sadly, this was not the first time a police officer came to my home and questioned me or my family about some other completely false accusation made by people who were against me politically.

At one point during my second campaign for reelection, a kooky supporter of my opponent started circulating an altered image online of my face in a full Nazi uniform. I'm no Nazi and it made zero sense.

But to this person, it was a way to attack me. I can tell you that even though I laughed when I first saw it, and I pretended I didn't care, I did. It hurt badly. I knew that it was complete bullshit. However, the fact that my friends and family, and associates of myself and my wife and our children also saw it, was devastating.

The same people would drive around town and either steal my yard signs, or paint a big bright red X over them. Nice, huh?

You have to have a thick skin to be in politics. I remember going to the grocery store and seeing people look or stare at me and wonder if they were thinking, "That's that asshole councilman who voted to spend my tax dollars on a youth baseball field. I hate baseball!"

When the reality was the person was probably looking over

my shoulder at the deli counter and I was just being paranoid. It got to me. It began to crush me.

Imagine how this felt.

In the last three weeks before my second election my wife and I noticed that my opponent was driving past our house at least 20-30 times a day. It was obvious he was campaigning to my neighbors. But what was he doing and saying exactly?

As we found out, it wasn't nice. Here's basically what he was telling people to their faces.

"Kukral and his wife are phonies, you know that, right? They are bad parents who have horrible, unruly children. He's a terrible person, both him and his wife, and his kids. Everyone in the community hates them. He lied to you about who he is. He's a thief and a liar who is ruining this city."

All of which was completely ridiculous and untrue of course.

When friends and supporters called us to tell us what he was saying we were BLOWN away. Never, in a million years, would I say anything like that about another person, for any reason, election or not.

I want you to imagine how that felt to have a person go to all of your neighbors and talk about you and your family like that? People who you see every day when you're getting your mail or mowing your grass. People you see at the grocery store or at a school event. Your kids' teachers! Your kids' coaches! Ugh.

Tell me it wouldn't bother you. It was terrible and soul crushing.

Then the most punishing blow came when the opponents of myself and the others who I was aligned with were mercilessly attacked in an 8-page fake newspaper called "The Seven Hills Election Guide 2017."

Looking back on it now, I have to laugh. At the time, seeing an entire fake newspaper, distributed to every home in your city that completely obliterates you and all of your hard work and good name with lies and bullshit, was devastating.

When I saw that I knew my time in politics was over.

Lesson learned. Politics isn't for people like me. I cared too much and actually wanted to do too much. And as you will read later on in this book, we don't trust politicians, and we certainly don't look to them for change any longer.

I now try to affect change by donating more of my time, money and resources to local, non-political organizations that my family and I care about. Organizations and causes that share our values and beliefs.

If you would like to learn more you can visit my website where you can watch a video my daughter made about how to create homeless care kits. As a family we prepare these kits which include items like socks, deodorant, snacks, toothpaste and toothbrushes, etc... Then we distribute them to people in need, together.

* * *

Sometimes Just Being Different Makes You Unskippable

When I ran for office I could have easily tried to stand out by walking door-to-door wearing a bright orange jumpsuit with a giant foam finger that said, "Vote for Jim". However noticeable I would have been, that tactic wouldn't have gotten me elected. My first book, Attention!, covers this entire argument from start to finish.

But sometimes just being different is enough to stand out and build an entire Unskippable brand. Or at the very least, an attention-getting marketing campaign that gets people talking, and hopefully, buying as well.

To truly understand business you must understand the customer, and more specifically, why people buy. Every book about sales will tell you the same thing. Consumers make purchasing decisions based upon emotions and need before they get to the "free shipping" argument.

Humans are emotional. We make emotional decisions. We make irrational decisions. We pay attention to things that are fake, and ignore things that are real. We are beyond flawed, which is what makes us human and is simultaneously our greatest strength. We feel before we think.

What makes you Unskippable?

I'm going to keep hammering this question on you for this entire book. Because that's why you're reading. You know that you MUST stand out. You know that if you don't do something you're eventually going to get beaten by a competitor, or worse, never grow your business and fade away into being just average.

I want you to stop for a second and get out a piece of

paper. On that paper I want you to write down what it is about your business or marketing that is Unskippable.

You are not allowed to use things like "we're cheaper" or "we're faster". In other words, don't use the same things everyone else can say.

If you can't put at least one thing on that sheet of paper, you've got some work to do. Keep reading.

$$* * *$$

Unskippable Brands In Crowded Spaces Differentiate By Simplifying

I really don't know anything about wine. I'm a wine idiot. And I certainly don't spend much money on my wine purchases. In fact, when I shop for wine I'm looking for inexpensive, good tasting wine that is a step above the bargain basement cheap wine you find on the bottom shelf that comes in a box.

But, that doesn't mean I'm not like everyone else, and I probably choose my wine based on the label or name. Let's be honest, we all do it.

At the end of the day, even wine experts say that you shouldn't care about the brand or price. You should only care that you like it. If you can find something cheap that you enjoy, bottoms up. I agree.

However, that doesn't change the fact that wine is an insanely competitive business that relies on branding to drive awareness.

Wine.net did a survey of 2,000 wine drinkers about their

buying and consumption habits. They asked them to choose between three bottles of red wine and three bottles of white wine without providing any information besides images of each bottle.

Wine.net also asked them why they made their decision. Was it the label? Was it how expensive it looked? Was it the shape of the bottle? The results were that 82 percent admitted they made their selections based on the appearance of the labels. 82 percent!

But as you will read further in this book, times are changing, and consumers are looking for bigger reasons to become loyal customers.

Enter a new breed of company called Obvious Wines.

The concept of Obvious Wines was obviously smart to me. Basically, they're de-snobbifying the wine business by creating simple, yet delicious, smartly-packaged wine that explains the wine to you on the label.

Their tag line is "Because you shouldn't need a PhD to drink wine."

Exactly.

One of the biggest issues with wine is that the vast majority of wine drinkers don't know anything about wine. But Obvious Wines spells it out for you. Literally. Here's what's on the label.

First off, they don't have pretentious names; it's about as generic as you can get. They are named by number and taste.

#01 is called "Dark & Bold".

#02 is called "Bright & Crisp".

#03 is called "Light & Lovely".

And #04 is called "French & Bubbly".

Pretty simple and self-explanatory, right? So, you're shopping for wine, and you're looking at a wall of hundreds of wines and you're thinking to yourself, "I have no idea what to buy. But, I do know what kind of taste I like." You come across Obvious Wines and instead of "Merlot" or "Riesling" they offer you "Dark & Bold" or "Bright & Crisp".

You keep thinking in your head. "I like dark wine. I like bold wine. I also like bright wine and crisp wine." Or maybe I don't. Maybe I like light wine?

Well, I could take a chance on this fancy label wine that does NOT describe to me what the wine is like, OR I could just buy this one that spells it out for me.

All things being considered, I believe that a consumer will choose the one that spells it out for them more often than having to guess, especially in a sea of choices that makes your mind spin.

Imagine you're heading out to enjoy dinner at a friend's house and you want to bring wine. Your first instinct might be to just choose one with a fancy label, but again, you have no idea if that wine is going to be good or if your friend is going to like it. With the way that Obvious Wines spells it out, you lessen the risk.

The label on the back of each bottle of Obvious Wines takes it even a step further. They explain exactly where the wine was made and the mix of the wine. For example, #01 was made in Bonjour, California, from American grapes from PASO Robles, CA. It's a "French Bordeaux style blend of 2 varietals: 51% Cabernet Sauvignon and 49% Merlot."

#01 also explains what wine is best to serve with what food. This particular blend is great paired with poultry, tacos and cheese.

Next up on the label tells an even deeper story that belief-driven buyers (more on them later) will love even more. #01 is made from "advanced farming methods to sustain environment. Example? 100% of winery power is solar panel generated."

Boom! How many wines tell that story? Nobody does. That's yet another reason why Obvious Wines is Unskippable.

Finally, there is a scale of flavor that shows how the wine ranks with taste with descriptors like Sweet, Body, Fruits, Acidity, Tannins and of course, Alcohol Level.

Key Point: Becoming Unskippable isn't always about having the fanciest label. Instead, it can be about demystifying and explaining who you are and why you are different.

* * *

How'd You Like To Be A Repairman These Days?

It's 1990. You wake up and realize that your dishwasher is broken. You pull out the manual and begin the process of trying to troubleshoot it.

Unfortunately, the type is so small you can't read it, and there's nothing in the manual about how to fix it. But you do find a customer service number.

You call. After an hour on hold you finally get ahold of a person that is less than helpful. They give you a few ideas of what you could try. You try them, but without actually seeing what the person is describing, you can't figure it out.

Ugh. Now you're late for work and the dishwasher is still broken and you HATE doing dishes by hand.

That's when you pull the Yellow Pages out from the drawer under the counter. Remember the Yellow Pages? For the younger people reading the Yellow Pages were gigantic yellow books full of listings for businesses and they were the only way to look up information. Remember, this was before the Internet.

ABC Repair is the first place you call (they have the biggest ad, a full page), but they don't pick up. The message says they're closed for the night. You should have called earlier. The next place, Zito's Appliance Repair, answers and they're super nice. You have a nice conversation with Zito's daughter, who tells you that her dad is extremely busy this week, but he can probably come and take a look at it in a few days, maybe more.

You ask Zito's daughter to schedule an appointment and you hang up. Now you take all the dirty dishes out of your dishwasher and wash them by hand in the sink and put them away.

Then it's time to cook dinner. Because you hate washing dishes, you decide it's pizza night. Great, the Yellow Pages are still on the counter so you look under "P" for pizza and call for a delivery.

Six days later Zito shows up fix your dishwasher. Finally!

Zito hands you a bill. It was $349 for the part and another $159 for the service. That brings you up to $508 in total, plus all the money you spent on pizza and Chinese food, and having to wait almost a week to get it fixed.

Ugh, what did you do to deserve this? At least you can cook tonight.

Fast forward to 2019

Your dishwasher breaks. While standing in front of it, you pull out your phone and type in "how to fix a Bosch dishwasher" on Google. The first result comes up with a video entitled "Solved: How to fix a Bosch dishwasher".

You hit play. It's three minutes long. After sitting through the Unskippable five-second ad, you watch about a minute and a half and learn that if you just remove the drain mechanism, clean it out and hold the start button for three seconds, it will probably fix itself.

So, you try it. It's now been about a total of three minutes or less since you began this investigation, and your dishwasher is working perfectly. You get to work early. You cook that night. All is well in the world.

Poor Zito. He's retired now. Business just wasn't what it used to be.

Of course, there are still repairmen. But they're only needed for the problems you can't fix yourself because of the Internet.

Now let's imagine that Zito's son takes over the business. He's not getting as many calls as he should. It's getting harder to compete for the limited amount of business available.

He tries Google and Facebook ads with limited results. It seems like he can never break through all the competition from giant nationwide repair businesses who can outspend him 50 to 1.

Zito's son is about to give up until the day his daughter convinces him to start making videos about his repair jobs. She goes with him on a few jobs and films him with her iPhone.

In the first week, she uploads three videos to Youtube showing how her dad fixed three different brands of dishwashers. She filmed, edited and uploaded each video from her phone without any training. At the end of each video she puts Zito's phone number and Facebook link.

About a week later, Zito gets a call from a person who says their dishwasher was broken, and despite every attempt to fix it themselves by watching Youtube videos, they came across his video and decided to call.

Zito's son drives right over, and sure enough, the customer's problem was something that had to be done by a professional. He fixes it and says it'll cost $75.

The customer doesn't have checks, and no cash on hand,

however, he is willing to pay by Venmo or PayPal. Zito's son gives him his PayPal email and gets paid right on the spot.

Not a bad gig if you can get it Zito's son thinks. They called me. The job took 15-minutes and I got paid on the spot.

Zito's son then hires his daughter to come on certain jobs with him and film more videos. He triples down on videos and over time has uploaded hundreds of videos of him fixing every type of dishwasher known to man, with every problem you could ever think of.

The calls keep coming and the video views keep growing. In fact, Zito's son is so busy now he has to hire a second repairman because he doesn't have time to do all the work.

About six months later Zito's son realizes that he's got close to half a million views on his videos. A while after that Zito's son gets a call from an executive working for a very prominent dishwasher manufacturer.

They want to discuss paying Zito to sponsor his videos, as well use him to be their "Certified Repair Spokesperson" on social media. They offer him a contract for $3,000 per month to sponsor all his videos, and give him a $25,000 a year celebrity endorsement fee to be the face of their social media repair presence.

Unskippable Companies Break Free Of The Yellow Pages Mentality

Zito's son became Unskippable. Why?

Because he realized, albeit by accident, that the Yellow Pages mentality of the past does not work in today's world.

It used to be that you'd buy the biggest Yellow Page ad and the calls would come in. That was all you had to do. It was a good system. An easier system. In a world that was much simpler.

But those days are long gone. Perhaps you're still stuck in this mentality in your business and marketing? It's time to break that.

And no, just because you do Facebook ads or you spend some money on Google ads does not mean you're still not thinking in the Yellow Pages mentality.

In fact, it means you're still stuck there. Why? Because you're still focusing on "buying ads" as your main marketing strategy.

Mass market companies like Coca-Cola, McDonalds and General Motors are still stuck in this mentality with TV ads. 1. They have a lot of money. And 2. They are scared as all heck to stop spending all that money because maybe their profits will drop.

But their ads are skippable, even the most emotional ones. Rarely does a commercial they produce create emotion so well that it moves the needle on sales. And the cost of attempting to produce one at that level could be millions. A horrible return on investment to say the least. Yet they can't seem to break free from it.

You can though. You have to.

Does buying ads work? Yes, of course it does. Should it still be a big part of your marketing plan? Yes, of course it should.

But does buying ads really make you Unskippable?

Remember, nobody wants ads anymore. They want to skip them. And you can make your ad the most clever ad in the world, but it's still an ad, and people still want to skip it.

Do not forget that. It will serve you well.

And remember this. When you're focused on ads, you're not innovating.

So, what do you do? Well, that's what we're going to continue to uncover in this book. Keep reading, and get inspired.

Unskippable Brands Don't "Kill" Competitors, They Disrupt Poor Experiences

Amazon isn't killing retail. What's killing retail is that nobody wants to go to the store any longer.

Plus the fact that Amazon has conditioned us that we can just click a button and have anything we want sent to our front doorstep in 24 hours or less.

Heck, you can buy a house on Amazon now, anywhere from $5,000 to $50,000! They're prefabricated and come with free shipping to your "door" in 3-5 weeks, or less.

Let's just admit it. People don't want to leave their homes to buy stuff, even houses! That's the disruption that we all need to understand, and the companies that are making it easy for them to not have to do so are winning, big time.

Ever go to buy razors? You walk into Walgreens or Target and you have to find the razor aisle. Then you have to scurry to try and find some sales associate to unlock the case and give you your 10-pack of $30 razors.

Now you've wasted at least an hour of your time driving to the store, and having to find someone in the store to let you buy them. Then you have to drive home.

Or, you could just go to Harrys.com or DollarShave-Club.com and order them and have them at your doorstep the next morning - at half the price or less.

That's a disruption, and that's why Gillette is running scared.

The Internet Advertising Bureau (IAB) notes that Gillette's share of the U.S. men's razors business dropped to 54 percent in 2016, from 70 percent in 2010. Meanwhile, the combined U.S. share of shaving upstarts Harry's and Dollar Shave Club rose to 12.2 percent, from 7.2 percent, in 2015 alone.

Why? Because given the choice of having to go to the store and have the Walgreen's sales associate have to unlock the case and get your razors, or being able to just click a button on a website and your razors appear at your door a day later... well, it's pretty obvious.

Peloton is a company that sells stationary bikes with an online video screen. You may have seen their ads online or on TV, if you haven't skipped past them. Peloton charges you $39 a month to "ride online" with their trainers. And don't forget you first have to buy the $2,000-plus bike first!

They currently have over 1 million people who pay those fees. You can do the math ($39 a month x 1 million); it's insanely profitable. The company is now valued at over $4 billion.

But why? Why does a person pay all that money to ride a bike in their home when they could just get a Planet Fitness membership for $10 per month?

Because they don't have to leave their homes. Because it's a "hassle" to have to drive to the location, check in, find a machine, lock up your valuables, etc.

Because they don't feel judged in the privacy of their own home. Because the gym, for most people, is a poor experience.

Others are catching on. Mirror.co is a Peloton competitor that reminds me of a futuristic scene from a movie. It's a giant vertical "mirror" screen/monitor that you hang up or lean up against a wall that you stand in front of and do workouts with other people. It looks like a giant smart phone on your wall.

Like Peloton, you subscribe monthly ($39/month) for unlimited access to classes with instructors, and you can even schedule workouts with your friends. It syncs to your smart phone and even let's you take a selfie of yourself at the end which you can share to social media to tell the world you just worked out. You workout people know you love to do that!

Oh, and like Peloton, you have to pay for the device. The

Mirror costs $1,495. Do the math. You're spending $39/month, plus the cost of the screen, because you don't want to leave the house.

On the website they pitch it as "The future of fitness is at your place." In the video promoting the device they say, "No waitlist. No crowded parking lots. Just your home, the Mirror, and you."

Yeah, they get it. Are you starting to?

Walmart is currently offering grocery delivery right into your fridge, even if you're not home. In an article on MarketWatch, Chief Executive Doug McMillon said, "Once we learned how to do pickup well, we knew it would unlock the ability to deliver. What if we put their groceries away inside their kitchens or garages? Imagine keeping homes in stock like we do stores."

So now you're about to be able to completely skip the grocery store, and have the option of someone who will bring your groceries and put them in your fridge for you.

What's next? They cook and taste it for you too?

The point is, there are people so busy, and so bothered by the fact they have to go to the grocery store, that they're willing to let a stranger into their home and stock their fridge for them.

As if Amazon hasn't disrupted the world enough, now they're taking on the trillion dollar world of pharmacies and prescription drugs. They just introduced a new service called Amazon PillPack Pharmacy that shows, once again, that people simply want better experiences.

From the website, "Switch to a simpler pharmacy today. We're a new kind of pharmacy. We package your medication, and deliver it directly to your door. No more waiting in lines. We'll auto refill it and send it in daily dosage packs."

What sounds better? Going to your local pharmacy, or this?

Are your teeth crooked? Is your smile not what you want it to be? Well, you have a choice if you want to fix it. You can schedule an appointment at your local orthodontist and sit in her chair and have a technician stick sharp and uncomfortable tools in your mouth to ultimately measure you for braces or a retainer.

Or, you could simple click on over to SmileDirectClub and sign up online. They'll send you a measurement kit to your house. You follow the instructions, then send it back in. Then a technician will create a 3d map of your mouth and create a custom plan and device that will fix your problems. Then they'll send it to you and you do it yourself, at home.

Oh, and it's a third of the cost of going to the orthodontist. Which one sounds better?

Looking for a new car? Studies have shown that the vast majority of us are first doing the research online for what kind of car we want. When we find the make/model/color of the car we want to buy, we can either head to a car dealership, or we could simply order it online.

Websites like Carvana.com will not only give us financing online, but when we finally order the car we want, they'll have it delivered to a Carvana "vending machine" near our home. That means you can just walk up to the kiosk, put your code in, and your car will come down off the rack and you can drive it home.

Carvana.com is disrupting the car dealership model because nobody enjoys the experience of buying a car from a dealership. Nobody wants to deal with salespeople.

Nobody wants to hear "Let me go check with my manager on that price". Nobody wants to have to sit in the dealership cubicle for hours signing paperwork. Nobody wants to feel like they're being pushed to upgrade to more features and incur bogus fees for paperwork processing.

Buying a car from a dealership is a crap experience, across the board. With Carvana you do it on your own time, without all of those poor experiences, and that is why they will eventually win in that industry.

They disrupted the poor experience.

Carvana is now taking it to the next level. Want to sell your car? Talk about another terrible experience we all have to deal with. Carvana wants to change that too. Now you simply go to their website, input your license plate number, and get an estimate (cost) on the value of your car. Then just click a button to list it for sale with them. If it sells, Carvana will send a truck to your home to pick it up and cart it away, and send you a check. Easy peasy.

Gut check: What poor experience can you disrupt in your industry to make yourself Unskippable?

Let's say you have 10 competitors. Hopefully by now you've analyzed their business models and their marketing and processes. If you haven't, then you better get to it! But if you have, you need to stop thinking about how to compete on things like cost, or speed, but instead think about how to make a better customer experience.

Here are some more examples to get your juices flowing.

When you think of a bank what do you think of? You think of an intimidating, secure, unfriendly building. You walk in and there's an armed guard standing at the door. There's a formal line roped off for you to stand in to wait your turn for the privilege of accessing your money.

Then when you get up to the counter, you feel like you're dealing with an enemy, not a friend. You just want to make sure you don't screw something up or act the wrong way that makes you look suspicious. It's unpleasant in general, to say the least.

I'm forty-seven years old, so I'm used to this because that's how banks have always been for me. But imagine yourself as a 25 year-old just getting out of college who is about to choose a bank that they could potentially bank with for the next 50 years of their life.

Does that 25 year-old want to do business with the bank their parents do business with, or do they want to do business with a bank that has a better experience?

* * *

Unskippable Brands Understand Consumer Expectations & Deliver Experiences That Purposely Attract Lifetime Customers

Capital One, one of the largest banks in the world, is redesigning their locations to be more like hotel lobbies or coffee shops. There are snacks, and beverages. The layout is open and welcoming, with couches, comfy chairs and work-stations.

It's a pleasant experience. You feel like you can walk in and hang out. There's free Wi-Fi, and no pressure or intimidating and unfriendly employees. It's a pleasant experience that you can enjoy.

Have you ever enjoyed going to your current bank? Really enjoyed the experience?

"There's one by my house and I've been to it. It's like a coffee shop/bank/hangout/entrepreneurial space. It's awesome and that is a much better experience," says professional keynote speaker and best-selling author Andrew Davis.

"And I can see myself sitting there if I was an entrepreneur starting up a business, drinking my coffee, doing my work in the morning. If I have a question about getting a business loan, where's the first place I'm going to go? To the counter that's right over there. That's a great experience and I love it."

Expectations. That's what you are fighting against. Let's say you're a traditional mattress company. The expectation of the consumer is that you need to lay down on a mattress to make a purchasing decision. Why? Because that's how it's been done forever.

You see commercials all the time showing people testing out mattresses in a showroom. I guarantee you've gone mattress shopping and tested a mattress out. I've done it, and I know for a fact that in the past I would have never bought a mattress without testing it out first.

Do I really need to? I know I don't want to. But I've been scared to do it a different way because of the risk. I don't want the risk of ordering a mattress sight unseen, having it delivered, getting it up the stairs and into my bedroom, then laying down on it and finding out it's not comfortable.

That's real pain. Pain of time, energy and money.

But there's also other pain associated with that traditional buying process. There's the pain of having to find a mattress store near me. The pain of checking their hours and finding time to drive there. Then there's the pain of having to have the salesperson pounce on me the minute I walk into the store.

Next there's the pain of the salesperson trying to upsell me to a more expensive mattress out of my budget. Then the pain of having to wait for the salesperson to talk to their manager and see if they can get you a better deal.

Finally, there's the pain of having to sit down and fill out the paperwork and choose a delivery date.

Now the question becomes; which pain is worse? The risk/pain of ordering the mattress online, or the risk/pain of the retail experience?

This is what I call the Unskippable Pain Index. It's the pain ratio in the customer's mind of expectation vs. pain.

The numbers don't lie and the examples don't either. Casper catapulted to the top of the online mattress business by capitalizing on those pain points of the consumer. They are disrupting an industry that's projected to be worth $43 billion by 2024.

Sure, Casper has retail stores, but they're not full of pushy salespeople with clip-on ties trying to make a commission. They are called "The Dreamery" where customers are encouraged to come in and actually take naps. But you don't have to nap. You can just order your mattress online and have it delivered to your home in a big box.

Then, you can sleep on it for up to 100 days to see if it's a good fit. If it's not, just throw it back in the box and here's the best part, they'll pick it up. You don't have to try and take it down to the post office and put a roll of stamps on it.

That's a funny mental image.

Let's get this straight. They'll deliver it to your home. You can sleep on it for three months and if you hate it, you get your money back and they'll come pick it up?

Yep, that's Unskippable right there. Tell me why you'd want to do it the old way?

Enjoy Technologies takes it a step further. Want to buy an iPhone? Well, you have choices. You can go to the Apple store and have a generally pleasant experience, but you still have the pain of setting up an appointment, driving there and the stress of getting there on time and then waiting in a very busy store for them to get to you.

Or, you could go to another retail store like Best Buy or even a cell phone provider and buy your new phone.

But what if you could order your iPhone online and what if a company like Enjoy personally delivered it to your home by a trained person who won't just leave it on your doorstep, they'll come in, help you unpack it, transfer all your files and show you how to use it? For free.

Yes, it costs nothing more to have it delivered by a person that will come into your home and actually help you set it up!

Yeah, that's pretty Unskippable isn't it? And that's the future.

Don't believe it? Need more proof?

Renee Dua and Nick Desai founded Heal in 2014. It's an app that allows patients and caregivers to hail a doctor seven days a week, from 8 a.m. to 8 p.m., for pretty much any service a primary-care physician can provide.

Visits are covered by insurance or a flat $99 fee. Medical assistants, who are Heal employees or contractors, drive the docs to their 12 to 14 appointments a day in company-provided cars. In the homes of chronic disease patients, the company installs a "Heal Hub", a device that checks vital signs and has a two-way radio that connects patients directly to a doctor.

Once again, if you have the choice to either call the doctor and get on their calendar and then have to wait for the appointment, drive there, sit in the waiting room reading a dumb magazine or playing games on your phone, then waiting some more, until you finally get in to see the doctor. Meanwhile, you've had to call off work for a half-day.

Or, you go to the Heal app, set up your appointment, and the DOCTOR COMES TO YOUR HOUSE.

Which one do you want?

Because again, the experience of going to the doctor is not a joyful one. If only this could happen with dentists, right?

This is why retail is dying and everything, well, almost everything is being disrupted. Because people are now refusing (and don't have to) leave their homes for poor experiences. They've now got options that allow their new expectations to be met.

This is why the tow truck company that optimizes the customer experience using text messages and apps is going to win over the one that still relies on phone calls and paper invoices.

Eyewear is a $140 billion industry that was a borderline monopoly. Until a company called Warby Parker disrupted the model by allowing you to go online and find a few pairs of glasses you might like, have them sent to your home, you try them on, pick the one you like the best and ship the others back, for free.

Netflix didn't kill Blockbuster - late fees, the inconvenience of having to go to the store, and streaming media did.

Uber didn't kill taxi cabs. Waiting in long lines and inconsistent fares did.

Carvana isn't killing car dealerships, pushy salespeople and a bad customer experience are.

 "You can't look at the competition and say we're going to do it better. You have to look at the competition and say how you're going to do it differently." - Steve Jobs.

Again, what poor experience of your competitor can you make better by doing it differently? Because that's how you're going to become Unskippable.

Not ads, not taglines, not blog posts, not sales funnels, not chatbots - none of that stuff.

Let's say you're an accountant who does taxes for people and businesses. There are a million competitors all vying to steal your clients. Think about the experience you're providing for your customers, and think about their pain.

For 99 percent of us, we hate dealing with taxes. It's intimidating, confusing, bothersome and inconvenient. So how do you, someone who does taxes for a living, make a better experience for your customers, knowing all we just talked about?

How about this? Instead of forcing your clients to come to you, why not promise you'll come to them? Remember, people don't want to leave their homes. Promise them you'll make it easy on them and come over and get what you need from them. Then, go back to the office and do their taxes, but don't just call them and tell them to come and pick them up.

Instead, create an event called the "XYZ Accounting 'Taxes Are Done' Pickup Breakfast!" Cater the event at your office or rent a private room at a local breakfast spot. Invite your clients to come in and have a free breakfast while they pick up their taxes.

Turn an unpleasant experience into a pleasant one.

Create an experience that they look forward to every year, not one they dread.

Imagine the word of mouth they will give you to their friends about you. That's how this all works now - referrals.

People go on social media and say, "I need someone to do my taxes, who do you recommend?"

At this point a few things happen when someone asks that question.

1. They get no response because there is nothing Unskippable about their tax provider so they don't feel compelled to share.
2. They get a lame duck response like, "I use ABC Accounting. They do just fine."

Or, they give this response.

"You have to call my guys at XYZ Accounting. Not only do they make it easy by coming to your house to pick up your information, but every year they have this great breakfast event where you go and pick up your taxes and eat for free! It's over at Don's Breakfast bar in W. 130th, where they have those amazing pancakes. I look forward to it every year!"

Which one is Unskippable?

Let's try another example. Let's say you have a home remodeling company. Every day you compete for jobs in your neighborhood by showing up and giving quotes on redoing kitchens, bathrooms and decks.

You understand that your target customer is most often looking at price as the big decision. But you also understand that one of the biggest reasons you win more jobs than you lose is because you have a reputation for showing up on time, doing great work and also getting the job done as quickly as possible without causing too much disruption to the homeowner.

So, you put together an app that your clients can open 24 hours-a-day that shows daily updates, schedules, prices, work times, and more. They can even click a button and text the owner of the company, or the lead contractor on the job. And they can report something they don't like in the same manner.

This is actually a true scenario that my contractor uses. I was blown away by it when he showed it to me when pitching my bathroom remodel. He ended up being about 15 percent more expensive than the other quotes I had gotten, but I loved the concept of keeping me informed so much that my wife and I agreed it was worth the extra money.

In other words, he made his business Unskippable.

Remember, Unskippable businesses understand that complacency isn't sustainable. It's innovation and a willingness to think differently that keeps them alive and competing into the future.

Unskippable Brands Create Talkable Moments On Top Of Great Experiences

As I mentioned earlier, this is what Jay Baer's excellent *Talk Triggers* book (a must-read) is all about - creating talkable moments and experiences.

In a recent episode of Jay's YouTube series The Talk Triggers Show, Jay brought up some really powerful points about a doctor in Seattle who pioneered the procedure of "knife-free" vasectomies. DrSnip.com, or Dr. Chic Wilson, dominates the vasectomy business through differentiation and creative talk triggers.

From the episode, "I don't know everything, but I do know this. The more you try to fit in, the more your customers will try to tune you out. You need to differentiate your business so much where your customers want to do your marketing for you. Even in competitive situations where you actually have a true quality advantage."

Dr. Snip was first to market with a vasectomy procedure that did not require normal surgery, you know, with a scalpel. The procedure attracted many men who were deathly afraid of going under the knife, and his practice exploded, in a good way.

Soon many other doctors, not just in Seattle, but around the world, copied his procedure and started to crowd the marketplace. In other words, Dr. Snip no longer had a unique offering.

So what made Dr. Snip differentiate himself from the pack? As Jay points out, after a procedure each man is given an engraved silver pocket knife.

Jay continues, "The best talk triggers are experiences. They live in three dimensions, not just in two dimensions like on a brochure. Even when you're really better, it still pays to create conversations by doing something customers do not expect."

A pocket knife from Dr. Snip certainly qualifies as unexpected in my opinion.

Another great book titled *The Power of Moments: Why Certain Experiences Have Extraordinary Impact* by brothers Chip and Dan Heath also nails it. In the book they explore why certain brief experiences can jolt, elevate and change us, and how we can learn to create such extraordinary moments in our life and work.

Remember, not just work, in life too. Unskippable in everything.

From the book description:

While human lives are endlessly variable, our most memorable positive moments are dominated by four elements: elevation, insight, pride, and connection. If we embrace these elements, we can conjure more moments that matter. What if a teacher could design a lesson that he knew his students would remember twenty years later? What if a manager knew how to create an experience that would delight customers? What if you had a better sense of how to create memories that matter for your children?

This book delves into some fascinating mysteries of experience: why do we tend to remember the best or worst moment of an experience, as well as the last moment, and forget the rest. Why "we feel most comfortable when things are certain, but we feel most alive when they're not." And why our most cherished memories are clustered into a brief period during our youth.

Readers discover how brief experiences can change lives, such as the experiment in which two strangers meet in a room, and forty-five minutes later, they leave as best friends. (What happens in that time?) Or the tale of the world's youngest female billionaire, who credits her resilience to something her father asked the family at the dinner table. (What was that simple question?)

Many of the defining moments in our lives are the result of accident or luck—but why would we leave our most meaningful, memorable moments to chance when we can create them? The Power of Moments shows us how to be the author of richer experiences.

This is a good book.

What moments are you creating that make you Unskippable?

Or better yet, what moments is your competition creating that makes them Unskippable?

You can either choose to be the hunter, or the hunted. The hunter will create the most memorable experience, and that loaded weapon will always defeat the unloaded one in the field of battle.

One of the most fun examples given in this book is that of the Magic Castle hotel in Los Angeles. This is from the Inc.com article that references the book.

Los Angeles boasts plenty of terrific hotels. At this writing, the top three on TripAdvisor are the Beverly Hills Hotel, Hotel Bel-Air, and the Peninsula Beverly Hills. If you can get a room at any of them for under $700 per night, TripAdvisor says you're getting a "great value."

The fourth name on the list is the Magic Castle Hotel. You can snag a room there for $199, but TripAdvisor doesn't call that out as a great rate. The Magic Castle Hotel, as Chip Heath, the Thrive Foundation for Youth Professor of Organizational Behavior at Stanford Graduate School of Business, describes it, "is actually a converted two-story apartment complex from the 1950s, painted canary yellow ... [with] a pool that might qualify as an Olympic size, if the Olympics were being held in your backyard."

How does the Magic Castle Hotel maintain such an enviable TripAdvisor ranking among the 355 hostelries it lists in LA? In their new book, The Power of Moments, Heath and his brother, Dan Heath, a senior fellow at Duke University's CASE Center, trace it to the hotel's ability to create "defining moments." These moments, they say, are ones that bring meaning to our lives and provide fond memories.

One of those defining moments is the Popsicle Hotline. Visitors at the hotel's pool can pick up a red phone on a poolside wall to hear, "Hello, Popsicle Hotline." They request an ice-pop in their favorite flavor, and a few minutes later, an employee wearing white gloves delivers it on a silver platter, no charge. It's a small defining moment that doesn't cost much to produce, but has paid off for the Magic Castle Hotel.

It seems like a ridiculous thing to do. But is it really? I'm guessing if I was staying there I'd have found it to be a memorable experience for sure. Or as Jay Baer calls it, a Talk Trigger. Because I'd certainly be telling everyone about it if I experienced it.

I do a fun promotion to my email list every year, the day before Thanksgiving. I email tens of thousands of people and give out my cell phone number and say, "Hey, you busy today? I'm not. Here's my number. Call me and ask me a question, or a favor, or just say hi."

I get close to 500 calls most of which I can't answer because I'm already on the phone. Some people just call to say hello. Some call with a question or want some consulting. It's a lot of fun and I call every person back who left a message, sometimes weeks after.

But every year, without fail, I get at least one consulting job or speaking gig out of that email.

I don't know if this qualifies as a Talk Trigger, but I do

know that people talk about it, share it, and it gets me business. In recent years, a lot of people just text me instead because they don't like making phone calls.

What it all comes down to is creating defining moments for our customers that elevate the normal experience to an extraordinary experience.

Unskippable companies make this THE main focus of their brand and marketing strategy.

* * *

66 Think I was kidding about giving out my number? Go ahead, text me, right now!

I'm at **(216) 236-8294.**

If you are enjoying this book send me a text message with the code word "Unskippable".

You won't get a chat bot, or be added to any list. It's just a regular text, direct to me. Can't wait to hear from you.

* * *

Skippable Experiences Create Friction, Which Stops The Customer From Using The Product Regularly

The KonMari Method explains this perfectly. You may have heard of the hit Netflix show by Marie Kondo called *The Life-changing Magic of Tidying Up: the Japanese Art of Decluttering and Organizing.*

The best-selling book, and now show, has become a cultural

phenomenon, inspiring people who would not normally pare down their possessions to throw away bags full of excess stuff.

The book centers on Kondo's particular method of radically decluttering a home or office, popular with her clients and the many attendees of her seminars.

To overly simplify the KonMari Method, it's basically, if something doesn't bring you joy, then you don't need it, so throw it out.

Or in other words, for our purposes of this discussion, if a customer experiences friction while trying to use your product or service, they will probably fail to continue to use the product regularly.

Sounds about right, doesn't it?

What happens when you order a new tech device off Amazon and it arrives and the instructions are horrible and you can't figure out how to set it up and you can't just get it to work?

There's no joy in that, and in an instant you went from excitement to frustration and anger, which leads to bad reviews and in general bad word of mouth.

Why do you think Apple products do so well? Because they just work and that provides a joyful experience.

Bryan Eisenberg's book *Waiting For Your Cat To Bark? Persuading Customers When They Ignore Marketing* nails this.

From the book:

"The goal has been to remove friction from the sales process. Friction

results from the customers' experiences of cognitive dissonance, an inability to feel that the sales process alone has met their ultimate needs. The piece missing for customers is confidence—the lower the degree of confidence, the higher the friction. Smart merchants know the secret to success is not to make it easier for the seller, but to make it easier for the buyer.

The introduction of new technologies has always provided lubrication to ease the friction. Transportation technology, communication technology, and payment technology have all improved over the years. Those merchants who took advantage of the new technologies prospered. Those who pooh-poohed them were left behind..."

The experience economy, first identified by management thinkers, B. Joseph Pine II and James H. Gilmore is upon us. It signifies the final blow to the notion of mass marketing. Today, the experience of the product or service—the experience of the exchange itself—defines delight and ultimately spells success or failure for the business and the brand.

Experience is not objective. And it is your customer's perception of the experience that you must strive to improve. The more you reduce friction in your sales process, the more you accommodate your customer's buying process, the more confidence the customer gains, the better the customer experience.

The increased intimacy of that experience is what allows customers to ascribe a deeper connection and more value to products and services."

Again, Unskippable Products And Services Create Joyful Experiences.

Got a startup that sells fancy socks online? What your customer really wants to buy from you is joy of the comfort and showing off your socks to friends, not the actual socks themselves.

Do you purchase things that make you angry? You might, but you never buy them again. If you buy socks and they arrive and they aren't comfortable and they don't go on and come off easily, does that produce joy?

We don't actually buy what we think we buy. When you buy a diamond ring to get married, you're buying "forever". Nike sells "winning", not shoes and hats and golf balls.

What do you really sell? What joy does your customer experience when they unbox your item? If you can't answer those questions then you have some work to do. Because without that joyful benefit, chances are that customer isn't going to buy from you ever again.

It's all changing, and that's the disruption. Look what we're up against in the future.

Do you sell to younger audiences? NPR reports that young people are choosing minimalist lifestyles like co-living (where you live in a "pod" with others instead of an apartment) because "we are now moving into an experience economy rather than a possessions economy."

Young people have long chosen to rent coworking spaces and take rideshares instead of buying cars, now they want to just live in a big room with other people?

An article on Futurism.com entitled "The Future of Sharing Means You'll Never Have To Buy Anything Ever Again" says that:

"Assets of an American 29-year-old in 1960: a house with a yard, a car, a killer record player.

Assets of an American 29-year-old in 2018: a fold-up

bicycle purchased via Craigslist, a laptop, a pair of decent headphones, a smartphone with a cracked screen."

The Sharing Economy, which so many younger people have gravitated to, is basically a collaborative system where a group of consumers share access to the same goods and services, usually at the benefit of a lower cost and more convenience.

Why buy a car, or heck, learn to drive, when you can call for a Lyft ride? What's a better, more joyful, experience? Paying a yearly car insurance bill and registration costs and waiting in line at the motor vehicle bureau or just renting a car for your trip to the beach?

* * *

Joyful Experiences Are Unskippable; Everything Else, Is Not

It all sounds so ridiculous, or does it? Depending on your age and mindset, you could think either way about it. But it's the reality of what we're all facing as small business owners or marketing executives, or start-up CEOs.

I met a gentleman at a speaking gig that was "changing the world" with his "revolutionary" teeth whitening system. When I asked him what joyful experience his product created his answer was, "We really believe our system is easier than everyone else's."

When I pushed back and said that "easy" isn't enough, I got him to reveal his true end benefit, which was "people feel better about themselves and they smile more after they use our product."

Joyful experiences...

You know what keeps most people going in this tough world we live in? It's looking forward to joyful experiences in our lives. When you don't have anything to look forward to, what happens? You have nothing to live for, and you become depressed.

Try considering that line of thinking into your marketing. After somebody clicks the buy button on your consulting service, what happens next that creates joy? Do you send them an oppressive form they have to fill out to continue the opportunity to work with you, or do you create a joyful experience for them that justifies them just giving you their money?

This is why television as we know it is being disrupted. Do you realize there is literally a person who has a job at each major television network with the specific responsibility of programming their most popular TV shows up against other popular TV shows in competitive time slots?

Do you realize that they purposely program a show to go over by a minute so that if you're "DVR'ing" other shows those shows could potentially be cut off and not recorded?

What these networks don't understand is that all they are doing is making the experience of watching TV worse. So, in these actions, they are actually stopping viewers from enjoying the TV experience.

They even go so far as to program in commercials that mimic the style and content of the show you're watching. For example, if you're watching the show *Vikings* you might get a commercial that has vikings in it.

Why? Because that's the only way they're going to get you to stop skipping through the commercial they're getting paid so much money to show you.

But again, what happens when you stop the fast-forward only to realize it's just another commercial? You get upset and frustrated. There's no joy there.

* * *

Are you starting to get a feel for what being Unskippable means yet?

Is your head turning with ideas? You may not have it just yet, but keep reading, by the end of this book you will. If not, schedule a call with me and let's chat about it. Just go to www.JimKukral.com.

At this point I'd like to ask you to share this book with your friends and associates. Simply send out a Tweet or Facebook or Instagram message and let them know you're enjoying what you're reading. Be sure to use the hashtag #Unskippable. Thank you.

PART II: UNDERSTANDING TODAY'S CONSUMER & POLARIZED WORLD

> *"You will continue to suffer if you have an emotional reaction to everything that is said to you. True power is sitting back and observing things with logic."*

*D*epending on what you believe and read on the Internet, this quote was either said by Bruce Lee or Warren Buffett. Regardless of who said it, I can't think of a better quote to introduce what we're going to cover in this part of the book.

We've reached a tipping point with our emotions. Not just as consumers, but as marketers and business owners or anyone else who is trying to communicate with and persuade the people who buy from us. And that includes dealing with our friends and family, and our bosses and co-workers.

We've allowed our emotions to get a little bit out of control. Sure, we always had outrage and we've always felt like we need to stand up and support things we believe in. However, the new age of social media has taken this to the next level.

It's funny, there are over seven billion people on this planet, and the Internet has connected us all. Still, all we've really managed to figure out is that we all disagree on pretty much everything.

Of course that's not true (completely). I'm not a cynic by any means, and neither should you be. But I hope you get my point, which is that times have changed, and we've got to understand exactly where we all are now before we can even try to better understand and communicate with each other.

In this second part of the book I want to talk about several things that will hopefully give you a better understanding of how people in today's world think, react, learn, and of course, buy.

And those are:

Point 1: Trust & The Rise Of The Belief-Driven Buyer

Point 2: The New Rules Of Tribalism: If Your Brand Isn't In Our Tribe, We Don't Trust You, Or Buy From You

* * *

Point 1: Trust & The Rise Of The Belief-Driven Buyer

In 2018 PR giant Edelman released a report called "Earned Brand" in which they identified "Belief-Driven Buyers". In short, belief-driven buyers are consumers that expect brands to lead the movement for change and address critical problems.

The report states that, "Today more than ever, consumers are putting their faith in brands to stand for something. To do the right thing. To help solve societal and political problems. Whether people are shopping for soap or shoes, they're weighing a brand's principles as much as its products. Opting out of taking a stand is no longer an option. How can a brand best put its values into action?"

Think about where we are in today's world. Gone are the days when the media was the most trusted institution in the world. In fact, it's now the opposite. We don't know what, or who, to believe.

More than half of the world is completely disengaged from "mainstream media" and trust in social media continues to falter. We don't know what's "fake news" and what is "real news" anymore.

On top of that, as if that's not scary enough, we trust government even less. Sure, we really never trusted politicians, but we used to trust government as a whole. They were like the wise, experienced mentor in your life that you could always turn to for advice and guidance, or to bail you out of a jam.

But over the past few years, that has changed, and something very interesting has happened instead.

Key point: Belief-Driven Consumers now believe that brands, not politicians, can save the world. And they're opening their wallets to those that have a product with a purpose.

Let's put it another way. Consumers now think that it's easier to get a brand to act on the issues they care about as opposed to electing another politician that can't get anything done.

They believe that by choosing a brand with a shared belief, they are effectively "doing their part" to change the world into what they think it should be.

This is, quite simply, a huge, powerful shift in thinking, and ultimately, a massive opportunity for brands that choose to take action on it.

And a massive missed opportunity for those that choose to not.

According to the Edelman survey, nearly two-thirds of consumers now identify themselves as a belief-driven buyer, and are more than willing to choose, or even switch to, or boycott a brand based upon its stance on societal issues.

The Edelman report, which surveyed more than 8,000 people around the world, stated that these belief-driven buyers now constitute a majority in all eight markets that were surveyed, which included China, U.S., Germany, Japan, U.K.

This is no fluke. And this isn't just millennials and young people. This is everyone. Sure, the 18 to 35 mindset on this leads the way at 69 percent, but the biggest rise (18 percentage points) was in the over 55 contingent. In addition, these belief-driven buyers are also the majority at all income levels.

What does this tell you? This tells you that a heckuva lot of people, across the world, with different ages and income levels, want you to give a crap about something they give a crap about.

And if you don't, they probably aren't going to choose you, and they certainly aren't going to advocate or become brand loyal to you.

Here are a few more conclusions from the report. When a brand supports their position on an issue versus staying silent, 51 percent of belief-driven buyers will be loyal, buying the brand exclusively and more often.

On top of that, 23 percent of belief-driven buyers will pay at least a 25 percent premium for a brand that speaks out with a position they agree with, versus one that remains silent.

And 48 percent of belief-driven buyers will advocate for or defend a brand, and criticize its competitors, if it speaks out with a position they agree with, versus a brand that remains silent.

Those are some powerful numbers and actions.

Belief-driven buyers not only think that brands can actually do more to fix the world, but that they have better ideas.

So now this huge shift is transforming marketing across the world, from the small business in your backyard, to the Fortune 100 billion-dollar conglomerates that sell you toothpaste, automobiles, pharmaceuticals, socks and pretty much anything else we consume.

Whether you're a real estate agent, or you own a pizza franchise, or your company makes shoelaces, on an emotional level your brand needs to stand for something if you want to do effective marketing and beat your competition.

It means your marketing team needs to stop having meetings about the next great television commercial you want to run during sweeps week. Instead start thinking about your brand story and how to effectively communicate what you believe to your customers that share those same beliefs.

Much has been written about Nike's now infamous "Believe in Something" campaign. It took the world by storm in 2018 by aligning the Nike brand with disgruntled and banished NFL star Colin Kaepernick.

Kaepernick became embroiled in the controversial movement of not standing for the U.S. National Anthem before he played an NFL game. He did it to protest social injustice. This created a firestorm of tribalism across the world and especially in the U.S.

The President even got involved tweeting out his opinion on the matter, which only escalated things. Tribes were formed, and suddenly you either belonged to one side, or the other.

Eventually, Kaepernick was cut from the San Francisco 49'ers and has not been resigned to another team since. In 2019 he settled with the NFL for an undisclosed amount. But the controversy continues on via social media and is perpetuated and fought over via tribal warfare on a daily basis.

It wasn't until Nike decided to sign Kaepernick to a multi-million dollar contract to be the face of the now famous

"Believe in Something" campaign that escalated the controversy to the next level.

I was speaking at an event shortly after this campaign launched and a man approached me after I finished. I noticed that he was wearing a shirt with a piece of tape over his left breast covering up something. Then I looked down and noticed his shoes, and there were pieces of duct tape covering the logos on the shoes.

I knew what was coming. I had just given a talk featuring the Nike story and this gentleman obviously wanted to talk to me about it.

Here's the thing. The man wasn't angry about it. He didn't want to burn his Nike products. He calmly expressed to me that A. He's never going to buy a Nike product ever again, and B. He already paid for these and they're comfortable. He figured he'd just cover up the logos to prove his point and show the world what he believes in.

Fascinating, to say the least.

The man was also very conscious about why Nike took such a stance. He understood he did not fit the targeted demographic of a loyal, long-term buyer for Nike, and that Nike frankly, did not care about what's in his particular wallet. Which is true.

When this campaign first arrived all the pundits were exclaiming about how dumb this move was for Nike. They said it would destroy the Nike brand and sales would go down.

They were right, sales went down for two days, along with

the stock price. But then after that, online sales went up 31 percent and the stock gained from where it was on the day of the announcement.

Why did so many people all of a sudden go buy Nike?

Because people support products and services that give them a better feeling about themselves. Key word: feeling.

What feeling do you evoke in a customer when they choose you?

Back in 1995, Nike released a campaign targeted at women called, "If you let me play."

The video showed women saying...

"If you let me play, if you let me play sports ...I will be 60 percent less likely to get breast cancer ... will suffer less depression ... will be more likely to leave a man who beats me ... less likely to get pregnant ... I will learn what it means to be strong. If you let me play ... play sports. If you let me play sports."

This stunning ad was not controversial because it had a great message that everyone could agree with. Also, because it was 1995 and we didn't have social media. If the same ad were released today we would ultimately get somebody, somewhere who would have had a problem with it.

The point is Nike has always known who their belief driven buyer is. In 1995 it was women, or rather, parents of girls. As a father of a daughter, how could I not be moved to support a brand that shared my common belief of wanting my daughter to be strong and successful?

Key Point: A brand can become Unskippable and grow when it acts to advance the interests of not only its customers, but also society as a whole.

McDonald's is being forced to "get it". They have to; their most loyal customers are dying off, and the belief-driven buyers of the world are taking their place.

From their website, "Today, McDonald's is announcing a policy to reduce the overall use of antibiotics important to human health, as defined by the World Health Organization (WHO), which applies across 85% of our global beef supply chain. According to the WHO, antibiotic resistance is one of the biggest threats to global health, food security, and development today. With our new policy, McDonald's is doing our part to help preserve the effectiveness of antibiotics for human and animal health in the future."

Let's not pretend this is more than what it is. We all know the facts. It's cheaper to raise cows with antibiotics. They grow faster and fatter.

Although I truly believe the fine people at McDonald's care about sustainability, I also suspect that if McDonald's didn't have to do this, they probably wouldn't. McDonald's is the largest single global purchaser of beef, so costs are definitely involved.

To their credit, they did a similar thing with chicken years ago when they refused to buy from chicken suppliers who use antibiotics.

Again, they know they have to do this, as do you. People simply care about things like this now.

* * *

Consumers Move To The Top Of The Food Chain

It used to be the other way around. Brands used to hold all the power over their customers.

The limited options for communicating your message allowed brands to control that message and ultimately pull consumers into their cult by simply beating them over the head with marketing messages.

If you wanted to be cool, you should smoke this cigarette. If you want to be happier, you should choose this floor cleaner.

We took a brand's word as the authority, and man oh man, that was such a happy time for businesses with deep pockets to spend on advertisements.

But then everything changed. Word of mouth used to be constrained to employees gathering around the water cooler at the office, or sharing a drink at the local pub.

Now word of mouth became social media where you could tell the world how much you love, or hate, something in an instant.

Brands went from being the hunter to the hunted, almost overnight. Consumers now sit atop the food chain, passing judgement through Tweets and videos and comments, and ultimately, their wallets.

Marketers panicked as did big business. Because they were no longer the authority where they could impose their will, they turned to attempting to engage with their customers through things like content marketing and better customer service, and it worked. And still does work in a lot of ways.

However, it wasn't long before consumers could easily sniff out the difference between content marketing and an advertisement. "Oh, you want to give me this free white paper that will tell me how to solve all my problems with my business, if I just give you my email address in return? Sure, I'll do that."

But then you get the white paper and start reading and realize it's just a big ad for the company.

Remember in the movie A Christmas Story when Ralphie got the Little Orphan Annie decoder ring and was so excited to read the secret message only to find out the message was an ad that said "Drink more Ovaltine?"

Yeah, that's kind of where things went and kind where some businesses still are and that stuff just isn't working anymore. In fact, it often has the opposite effect.

Yes, the power has shifted and it's causing a lot of chaos in the marketing world. I sat down and did an interview with Mark Schaefer, author of the book *Marketing Rebellion*.

Here's what Mark had to say on this topic.

"Our customers have become our marketing. We are in basically a loyalty-free world. Research shows that 83 percent of customers shop around. Only 17 percent are loyal. We try to create loyalty through content and try to engage, but research shows none of that matters. The customers are creating their own funnel.

There's only one single strategy that creates loyalty in

customers, and that is meaning, and values, and that's what's leading this trend. Price is less important, story is less important. They expect lower prices and free shipping, etc. What differentiates today is meaning. Do your values align with your customers?"

He continued, "Not everybody needs to take a stand, or be political. Sometimes you just want a hamburger because it tastes good. You don't have to take a stand. And you don't have to be polarizing.

Heineken created a powerful video called "World's Apart" that creates meaning in marketing and isn't polarizing. The most important things companies can do is not just talk about what you do, but show what you do. Show up where your customers are and show what you do. In general, people just don't believe companies nowadays."

When I asked Mark how businesses decide what they believe in, he said, "I think there are two different approaches. 1. American Eagle is the second biggest seller of denim in the country. Their marketing is 100 percent values-based marketing. They are against guns, proactive around LGBTQ issues, and even set up a foundation for protection of gay rights.

It's a very unusual way to sell jeans, isn't it? They have teenagers on their executive board to oversee that they don't say or do the wrong things. 2. Look internally and say "What is our why and how did we get here?" Legacy companies with strong owners start that way.

The risk is "are the values we have in tune with our customers and our employees?" It's a new day where values and meaning matter a lot, especially to young people. Don't be a lemming and follow some trend.

Be educated and make an informed decision. Don't just do something to follow a trend. The purpose of the corporation is to only make profits, period, is old school, and isn't true today."

* * *

Unskippable Brands Are Trusted, Duh!

As the world becomes more and more skippable, we have to ask ourselves why? A BIG part of that is trust. We all know it. Trust is the social contract that makes the world go round.

We trust that when we order an electric toothbrush on Amazon that it's actually going to live up to the reviews and recommendations from our brother.

We trust that the chef making us our lunch is really using the organic ingredients they claim on the menu.

Trust is the fabric of our every day social contract and without it, we are lost.

There are hundreds of books on trust, so I don't want to spend too much time telling you what you already know; That trust is important. Instead, let's talk about the current state of trust in today's world.

Because things have changed.

First off, in today's new world, the ramifications of breaking someone's trust can be devastating. We're no longer living in a world where you can misrepresent or even lie about what you do or what you sell and get away with it without the word spreading fast.

Consumers just aren't having it any longer, and they're MORE than willing to get on social media and tell every person they know about your bad service or lies. Again, we all get this. So let's move on.

I want to talk now about politicians because being a reha-bilitied politician has taught me a lot about how people think, react, buy and vote.

We hate politicians. We really do. Even the ones we like, we hate. It's true and it didn't used to be this way. Hubspot put out a chart about trust. Professions we trust.

According to the chart, we trust doctors, nurses and fire-fighters the most. Who wouldn't trust them? We trust teach-ers, of course. I'm the proud son of a public school teacher. We even trust dentists a little bit.

But you know who we don't trust so much? If you go down to the bottom of the chart you'll see that marketers and salespeople each bring in 3 percent, and professional athletes get 4 percent.

But if you keep looking down; You know what's coming. Car salesmen, lobbyists and, you guessed it, politicians come in at 1 percent each. Ouch.

Let's face it. Politicians suck, and people don't trust them. By the way, lawyers are at 12 percent and politicians can't even beat out baristas at 5 percent.

Yes, that 16 year-old girl serving your double half-caf

unicorn espresso with skim milk and no whip. That girl. She's trusted more than politicians in today's world.

That being said, why are politicians so good at getting your vote? Why then, are they so skilled at crafting messages and manipulating voters (customers)? Why do they keep getting elected term after term if everyone hates them so much?

It's obvious they're doing something right. Yes, we hate politicians, but man, they are good at a lot of things, and as a business owner, entrepreneur or executive, you need to understand how they get it done so you can make your business stronger and gain more trust with your customers.

Politicians try to separate themselves from their opponents on the issues, just as a business tries to separate themselves on benefits. But I've got news for you. Benefit-based marketing strategies aren't good enough anymore.

I'm gonna keep repeating this over and over until your eyes bleed. Sure, free shipping, discounts, and free white paper downloads still work for conversions. However, as I mentioned before, consumers expect those things and are moving beyond those as purchasing decisions.

Politicians know this and use it. At the end of the day it comes down, usually, to "which candidate would I like to have a beer with?" In other words, which candidate shares my beliefs and values? And that's why people vote.

It's also why people buy.

Dentsu Aegis Network, in conjunction with Oxford Economics, did a study in 2019 that polled 43,000 people about trust. The report states that nearly half of U.S.

consumers (45 percent) have taken steps in the past year to shrink their digital footprint due to lack of trust.

In addition, most Americans (60 percent) believe that social media has had a negative impact on political discourse. That's 15 percent higher than the global average.

In a NBC News/Wall Street Journal poll it was found that Americans feel pretty good about technology. But the same cannot be said about social media. The majority of Americans say they have positive feelings toward Apple (54 percent), Google (63 percent), and Amazon (65 percent).

But, less than a quarter of Americans say they have positive feelings about Twitter, and only 36 percent of Americans say they have positive feelings about Facebook.

A majority believe these platforms spread unfair attacks, rumors, lies, and falsehoods. Fifty-seven percent say the platforms divide us.

It's not bad enough we have an attention problem, we have a trust problem, and business as usual is not an option going forward. We have to find ways to embrace customers evolving attitudes so we can better meet their needs and not only get, but keep their attention and turn that into customer loyalty.

And only then can we become Unskippable.

Add this nugget on top of all of that (just to pile on): According to a Gallup report published on CNN.com, 2017 was the world's most miserable year on record. "2017 was the world's most miserable year in more than a decade, according to a survey of people's emotions in more than 145 countries.

People experienced sadness, stress, worry, anger and physical pain more frequently in 2017 than in previous years, according to Gallup's annual Global Emotions Report.

The results mean the world is more "negative" than at any point since the polling company started the study in 2005."

So not only do we have a trust problem, we have a LOT of miserable people. I'm confident those two things are related.

* * *

The Polarizing Effect Of Choosing A Side, Intentionally, Or Unintentionally

Let's say you're a business owner who built a brand through blood, sweat and tears. You're proud of your company. It's your baby. It's successful.

Now imagine you go to bed one evening and wake up the next morning to a global news story and hundreds of videos of once loyal customers now blowing up your product with dynamite and shooting it with high-powered rifles?

This is exactly what happened to Yeti coolers. Yeti coolers are really great coolers. Expensive coolers. You're gonna pay at least $300 for one.

It's not like the styrofoam ones you get from the grocery store. You know, the ones that break the minute you try to pick them up. You put too much ice in it, and it's full of your sandwiches and favorite beverages and it just collapses into a big pile in the back of your car.

No, Yeti is like the BMW of coolers. They have a great customer base too. They appeal to everyone. Outdoorsmen, families, soccer moms, you name it. Everyone needs a great cooler to keep their snacks fresh and their beverages cold.

But all of a sudden Yeti got the kind of publicity they didn't want. The National Rifle Association (NRA) created a firestorm when it announced that Yeti was no longer going to honor their partnership. It was a bogus story to get the large and vocal NRA base riled up.

Yeti says the story was spun the wrong way and, of course, they didn't mean anything by ending their association with the NRA. But in today's world, it doesn't matter.

The movement caught fire on social media. NRA supporters were literally blasting their Yeti coolers with high powered rifles and dynamite. A hashtag started called #thisyetiaintready that had thousands of tweets in 24-hours. Every main news network covered the story.

Meanwhile, Yeti's founder is probably wondering, "What the hell is going on?"

As a business owner you definitely don't want to ever ask yourself that question. Because if you do, you're in some deep trouble.

Then the Yeti competitors, one of them being Rtic, who were always playing catch up, noticed the weakness and piled on by launching a campaign saying they chose the side of the NRA. And guess what, their sales exploded.

It wasn't all bad news for Yeti. Unintentionally, those that approved of their stance and who had never purchased a

Yeti cooler before came out saying they were going to support the company and Yeti sales skyrocketed.

The moral of the story here is one bad move potentially alienated half of Yeti's customer base overnight, and opened the door for their competitors who were trailing behind to move in and eat up their market share.

If that doesn't keep you up at night as a business owner or executive I don't know what will.

We're a divided world. We're a divided country. The implications of potentially alienating half of your customers because of political position (intentionally or unintentionally) can be staggering.

So, you have some choices to make. You can shut up and not take a position on anything, or you can speak your mind and deal with the consequences.

People are exhausted by all the polarization going on in the world, even though they are opening up their wallets and making purchasing decisions based upon common beliefs.

In other words, consumers are saying one thing; yet doing something else, which is what makes where we are in the world a difficult time for marketers.

One thing is for sure, most of us are exhausted with all the fighting. Two-thirds of Americans consider themselves to be part of the "exhausted majority", which are people who share a sense of fatigue with our polarized national conversation. These people have a willingness to be flexible in their political viewpoints, but feel they have a lack of voice in the conversation.

This is another reason why so many people consider themselves to be belief-driven buyers. They feel they can affect change through consumerism, rather than relying on politicians and governments.

* * *

Point 2: The New Rules Of Tribalism: If Your Brand Isn't In Our Tribe, We Don't Trust You, Or Buy From You

Values-Based Marketing Takes Over

There's a new dating app called DonaldsDaters.com. It's mission is "to make America date again". They state on their website that, "Many on the Left chose party over love stopping any date if the other user is a supporter of our president."

Donald Daters CEO, Emily Moreno, said in a TV interview, "For many young Trump supporters, liberal intolerance has made meeting and dating nearly impossible. Support for the president has become a dealbreaker instead of an icebreaker. That's why we created a new platform for Trump supporters to meet people without being afraid of talking politics."

In this instance, an entire new business was created over one specific value: support for the current President of The United States.

Regardless of your political affiliation, you can see the draw in this type of polarizing differentiation. It just worked.

Imagine how difficult and expensive it would be to start a

new online dating company out of thin air and get it noticed and get new customers without some type of value-based hook that appealed to a specific audience? We're talking about a billion-dollar industry with gigantic competitors like Match.com and eharmony.com that have advertising budgets that will crush most competitors.

DonaldsDaters.com rose into success without any big marketing push - just a value-based concept that appealed to a very specific tribe. This couldn't have been done before the Internet, social media and the 24-hours news cycle. Today it's a perfect example of where we are and what can be accomplished if you choose a side and market it well.

* * *

Consumers Are Putting Their Money With Brands That Tug At Their Heart Strings

This goes way beyond political tribalism. Consumers are more informed and conscientious about the products and services they choose based on many different factors/causes.

This could be things like environmental concerns, or ethical concerns. For example, as in the case of Flex Watches, consumers are now making a decision to buy a watch because that watch supports Autism or Breast Cancer, over a watch that doesn't.

This is because the values of the watch company, the purpose of the watch company, and how you FEEL when you buy and wear the watch, are now more important than the watch itself.

This global shift in attitude and behaviors is not going away any time soon. Brands that begin to understand that they have to do more than just have a better price and product will win this battle. Brands that refuse to care about something will not.

What do you care about? More importantly, what does your customer care about?

Is it sustainability and protecting the planet? According to the Nielsen 2015 Global Corporate Sustainability Report, two out of three consumers will pay more for brands committed to sustainability.

Furthermore, sales of consumer goods from brands with a demonstrated commitment to sustainability have grown more than 4 percent globally, while those without grew less than 1 percent.

Just to make sure you caught the biggest point in that paragraph above.

They will PAY MORE.

Not just buy more, or become more loyal, but also pay more.

That's huge.

A large part of the world's population doesn't believe we have a problem with things like climate change, or believe that we need to do anything to protect the planet from annihilation. But just because they don't, doesn't mean there isn't a LOT of other people that do care.

They do, in a big way. These consumers truly believe they are being more responsible citizens of the world by supporting corporations that justify their beliefs. They check labels before they buy. They do their homework by looking at websites and doing research on how companies make and source their products.

These consumers also check out which organizations the brand supports through charitable contributions. They pay attention on social media and in the news. Then they form an educated opinion and boom, if the values line up, they're now a customer, for life.

This is how labels such as "organic" become so powerful. Organic has become synonymous with the concept of "I'm helping to save the world." But also, "this product is free of harmful chemicals that can hurt me."

Unfortunately, as many brands try and manipulate the consumer by throwing the word organic on a label and just hoping the consumer doesn't read the fine print.

That kind of thing may have worked before the Internet, but in today's world it does not. A consumer can easily research if a product is truly organic, or not.

Obvious Wines, which I talked about earlier in the book, is a great example of tugging on the heart strings of belief driven buyers with sustainability concerns. They show you (right on the label) where the grapes to make the wine are grown, and how the winery that grew the grapes was powered by wind or solar.

That means a lot to many people, and that's value-based marketing in a nutshell.

In the Nielsen 2015 Global Health and Wellness Report

they asked this question to 30,000 consumers in 60 countries.

"Thinking about the consumable brands you purchased in the last week, (such as food, drinks, toiletries, over-the-counter drugs, etc.), how much influence did the following factors have on your purchase decision?"

Here are a few highlights to underscore the point.

"62 percent are products that are made by a brand/company that I trust."

So two out of three consumers think brand trust is important.

How do you build trust? You are authentic and transparent in what you believe in. How? Why not just put it on the stinking label? Novel concept, right?

Maybe it's food sourcing that is driving your belief -buyer? According to the Nielsen Report, 82 percent of people now say they're willing on some level to pay more for healthier foods, with over a quarter reporting they were "very willing" to pay a premium.

The rising demand is characterized by natural simplicity, with buyers increasingly articulate about GMOs, additives and all the things they don't want in their foods.

Get it? Consumers give a "you know what" about this kind of stuff now. And it's not just Millenials and Gen Z.

Maybe you've written off all this woo-woo belief-driven buyer stuff because you personally don't believe it, and that your older skewed audience currently doesn't buy into it.

Maybe you're right, but here's a stat for you. Millennials are an increasingly large component of the workforce, on their way to 75 percent of the global workforce by 2025.

This is what they care about. This is what drives them to spend their money.

They're going to either buy from you, or someone who does care. They have very high ideals, with 87 percent of them believing the success of a business should be measured in terms of more than just its financial performance.

Of company attributes given by Millennials who do plan to stick around (be loyal customers), one of the most frequently cited buying factor as "a strong sense of purpose beyond financial success."

* * *

Unskippable "Luxury" Brands Do Better When They Rebrand Around Experiences & Utility, Not Logos/Social Status

I grew up in a world where driving a BMW or wearing a Rolex was a status symbol. I was told by society that if you had those things, you have "made it" and you were a person to be admired.

Oh, how times have changed.

There are still plenty of people that chase status symbols to bolster their egos and place themselves into the upper-echelon of their social and professional circles. However, what we're seeing now is that has become less important to consumers.

The Harvard Business Review came out with a study called, "Luxury Branding Below the Radar", where they looked at global trends like "inconspicuous consumption", which is a consumers' growing affinity for discrete rather than traditionally branded luxuries.

Giana Eckhardt, a professor of marketing at Royal Holloway, University of London, took a 2012 sabbatical to China and what she found surprised her.

"China was supposed to be the land of conspicuousness, but all of a sudden people were making fun of overt wealth and even taking the labels off their clothes," Eckhardt recalls.

Remember in the 1980's how you HAD to have an Izod shirt with the little alligator on it? That meant you were cool! If you showed up at school with a knock-off shirt with a similar looking lizard on the shirt you were made fun of.

Like it or not, that's how things used to work. But things have changed. Why?

Logos don't signal wealth the way they once did. From the HBR story, "Some companies, including Louis Vuitton, Michael Kors, Tesla, and Audi, have begun downsizing their logos, hiding them (putting them on the lining of a handbag rather than on the exterior, for example), or making them optional. Emirates airline has revamped its plane layouts and boarding system so that economy class passengers no longer see the perks afforded those in business and first class. Patrón has reduced the gilding on its tequila bottles, and Tiffany has dropped the spelled-out brand name from its fashion jewelry line in favor of a simple "T.""

Do you have a "luxury" brand? Are you seeing that smaller, niche brands are slowly, or quickly, taking market share from you? This is why.

What's really interesting is that this line of thinking is not just with fancy stuff like watches and handbags. It's now being accepted with items like groceries. Private-label brands like Costco's Kirkland Signature raked in nearly $40 billion in 2018, up 11 percent from 2017.

Kirkland's sales last year beat out Campbell Soup, Kellogg and Hershey put together. Wow! Because even with groceries, consumers are becoming brand agnostic.

It used to be that buying those knock off Cheerios called Wheateos was embarrassing, but not anymore. Again, why? I think we're just over it all. All the posturing and inflation of what society has told us was good, and what was not so good.

We no longer think we're a loser for saving some money, and that's a powerful habit change. And really, really bad news for big brands that built up years of trust and name recognition.

Consider this line of thinking if you're competing with a huge, well-known brand in your industry. It might serve you well. Now go get em!

Brands Are The New Elected Officials. And We "Vote" For Them Through Our Consumerism And Social Media Opinions

Our lives have become one big election for our personal brand. We are campaigning every single day on social media for what we believe in. From straight up political views, to what restaurants we like best, and yes, what brands we trust.

And here's the key. We want all of our friends to share our views, so we campaign them relentlessly to get them into our tribe and agree with us.

And if someone doesn't agree, they're the enemy. That's tribalism at its highest point.

"How dare you tell me that Pizza Hut isn't the best pizza? You must be an asshole! Unfriend me!"

This sounds completely ridiculous, but it occurs every single minute on social media.

We have become so tribal that we have decided that anyone who disagrees with our beliefs is the enemy.

True fans also bring true haters. It's the tribalism of it all.

We all need to realize something very important. And that is that we are all now living in a political reality show. All of us. Not just businesses. But you, personally, and yes, your business.

Like it or not, your business or career is now like being a contestant on Survivor. Think about it. Everything you do affects your chances of surviving this new world. Eventually, you're going to get eliminated or "voted off the island". It's just a matter of time.

Because life and business has now become political. All of it. There is no more separation.

Social media has become so ridiculous hasn't it? A popular thing now is to take a tweet from something you agree with and post the tweet on Facebook. Or post a response to someone with your retweet. It's like, you tweeted it already, but now you have to show who you tweeted it to, and your response on Facebook? It's redundant and exhausting.

Why do we do these things? Because we've become a narcissistic society where it's not enough to express ourselves. It's about winning, at all costs.

* * *

Ban, Blame, Boycott & Shame (BBBS)

A friend of mine who is a career politician once said to me, "I hate Mark Zuckerberg." Why? Because before we all had Facebook, we just hated everything and everyone else in private.

We've reached a level of mass awareness that, while powerful because we are more informed than ever, is also the direct cause of our differences and tribalism.

There are four reactions we now have when we find a cause to rail against. Because that's what humans do. We react. And now with social media and 24-hour news cycle that force feeds information down our throats like a fire hose, we are in a constant state of information overload to react to, all day, every day.

It never used to be this way. You used to get your news from the paper. Or the nightly news broadcast, and before that films or radio programs. Then you filtered that news thoughtfully and diligently and most of all, you kept your opinions to your small circle of friends, family and coworkers.

But not anymore. Now you're watching the news in real time, live, through a Facebook live video stream, or YouTube video. Now you're experiencing world events almost instantaneously. And you react.

Someone famous dies so you need to post that they died on your social media. An alligator attacked a man on a golf course in Florida. Oh boy! I need to share this with my friends!

Reactions are human, and let's be honest, they make us feel good. Sharing has become a dopamine hit similar to hitting the jackpot on a slot machine. We crave it, and we can't stop.

This is why it's so unbelievably scary to get caught up in political arguments or opinions as a business owner or executive. Because the world has changed. This is how we react now.

Our reactions are now ban, blame, boycott and shame, or as I like to call them, BBBS.

Let's face it, humans are reactionary. Social media has made it 1,000 times worse. These four things are basically what we've come to, and understanding these things will give you a better understanding of what we are all facing.

Ban - The company that disagrees with your religious beliefs? It's not enough that we don't just buy from them, we now have to see them banned! What does that even mean anyway?

Blame - Someone has to take the blame. It certainly can't be our fault, right? Because we're all perfect. It's as if we feel if we put the blame on someone else our lives would be better.

Boycott - It's not enough we have to try and ban them, the next level is to boycott them. Hashtags are created. Rallies are formed. Crowds are gathered at places of business.

Entire media campaigns and popular Internet memes are created all with the goal of trying to hurt a business, or person, that doesn't share our beliefs.

Shame - And here's the scariest one. It's not enough now to just ban, or boycott, or blame. It's now devolved into shaming. Accidents aren't considered accidents any longer. It's not possible that someone made a mistake, and now they must PAY FOR IT!

And things are about to get even worse. There are already apps where you can create fake text messages and Facebook messages and posts. Anyone can create a fake or parody account and use it against you, or your business.

Soon there will be software that will easily take a recording of a person's voice and auto synthesize that voice to say whatever you want it to say in the other person's voice.

Imagine how politicians will use this? Imagine how your competitors with bad intentions might use this? Even worse, imagine what a disgruntled customer might do with this?

Where do we go from here? I'll leave you with the immortal words of John Belushi's character Bluto from the movie Animal House. "Start drinking heavily."

* * *

Tribalism & How It Has Changed The World Of Business

If you think the tribalism we're seeing in today's world on social media and in society in general is new or unique, you'd be wrong. Ever hear of The Nika Riots?

January, 532 C.E., Constantinople. Scholars estimate that between 30,000 and 35,000 people were slaughtered in a deadly standoff between the Blues and the Greens, two factions of chariot racing fans that some argue held additional political and societal beliefs.

It is believed that the Blues were represented the ruling classes, and the Greens were the party of the people.

Sound familiar?

At first the Blues and Greens fought mostly about chariot racing that took place inside the Hippodrome, which in today's world would be like a sports stadium. Imagine two great tribal factions getting together inside one big building and fighting it out.

Not just being fans, literally fighting it out.

Note: We have this now, but it's on social media and

through the media. Fortunately we're not rioting inside Madison Square Garden, yet.

At first, the battle between the Blues and the Greens was all about chariot racing, but it all came to a head as each tribe continued to dig deeper and identify more with their tribal beliefs. It became about more than sport. It became about what, and who you believe, and if someone disagreed with you, well, then, they probably had to die.

Enter Byzantium's greatest, but most controversial emperor, Justinian (c. 482-565). Justinian historically favored the Blues, but as ruler, refused to pick a side when it came to taxation and other issues, which would prove to be a HUGE mistake for him.

Twenty-six new taxes were created, many of which fell, for the first time, on Byzantium's wealthiest citizens, or, the Blues, but also didn't go over well with the Greens. Nobody likes the tax man.

This sent shockwaves through the imperial city, which were further amplified when Justinian reacted harshly to an outbreak of fighting between the Greens and the Blues at the races of January 10.

Sensing the disorder had the potential to spread, and eschewing his allegiance to the Blues, the emperor sent in his troops to keep order. Seven of the ringleaders (Blues and Greens) in the rioting were condemned to death by Justinian.

The men were taken out of the city a few days later to be hanged, but the executions were botched. Two of the seven survived when the scaffold broke. The mob that had assembled to watch the hangings cut them down and hustled them off to the security of a nearby church.

The two men were, as it happened, a Blue and a Green, and thus the two factions found themselves, for once, united in a common cause. The next time the chariots raced in the Hippodrome, Blues and Greens alike called on Justinian to spare the lives of the condemned, who had been so plainly and so miraculously spared by God.

Soon the crowd's loud chanting took on a hostile edge. The Greens vented their resentment at the Justinian's previous support for their rivals, and the Blues their anger at Justinian's sudden withdrawal of favor.

Together, the two factions shouted the words of encouragement they generally reserved for the charioteers—*Nika! Nika! (*"Win! Win!")

It became obvious that the victory they anticipated was of the factions over the emperor, and with the races hastily abandoned, the mob poured out into the city and began to burn it down.

For five days the rioting continued as the city almost burned to the ground and an estimated 30,000 people (Blues and Greens) were killed. Right before Justinian sent in the troops to take order, the Blues and Greens attempted a coup to put their own leader in charge, but only because Justinian used extraordinary brute force by his army was he able to survive the attempt.

Justinian, *and this is important*, because he refused to take a side, was almost overthrown and a new emperor was almost put in place.

Let's repeat that. The emperor refused to support a tribe. Because of that, both sides turned on him and tried to replace him.

So, let's get back to today. You're not an emperor. You're not political in business, probably. At least you don't want to be, probably. You're saying to yourself, "We're just gonna keep our beliefs impartial and NOT choose a side. We're NOT going to choose a tribe."

I'm just gonna ask you this question and you need to give an honest answer.

Would you rather have 1 percent of the entire market, or 100 percent of half of it?

Because competing in today's world is harder than ever. As you have read in the stories about Yeti and Nike, choosing a tribe (intentionally or unintentionally) can, and does work. And as we have just read about Justinian and the Blues and the Greens, not choosing a side can be disastrous.

* * *

The Psychology Behind Tribalism

You get this, but you might just have to hear it again for it to take hold. Human beings become uncomfortable with people who we think are different than us. So by putting people around ourselves that see things the same way we do, we become more confident and powerful.

In Amy Chua's excellent book, *Political Tribes: Group Instinct and the Fate of Nations*, she argues that we are hardwired to be suspicious of others.

For example, in a study where young children were randomly assigned to red or blue groups, they liked pictures of other kids who wore t-shirts that reflected their own group better.

I was reading an article that was talking about how to truly be different you need to go beyond your tribe. That to "achieve anything worthwhile" you must transcend your tribe.

These are good thoughts, and on a 40,000 foot view of the current landscape of human society, they really make sense. I question the reality of them however, especially when it comes to business and branding.

My Friend Frank

Let's say you're a financial advisor like my friend Frank. You take other people's money and invest it and take care of it for them. They give you their nest egg and trust that you are going to nurture it and make it grow.

We're talking millions of dollars here, not pocket change.

So if you're Frank, and you're relatively new and haven't spent decades building up a brand and trust in your field, how do you get someone to trust you enough to give you all of their money to invest and take care of?

As you can imagine, it's not an easy ask. You're not going to make a Facebook ad and attract a customer. You're not going to cold call them. So how do you earn their trust?

This is the problem that Frank came to me with years ago.

"Jim, I'm getting nowhere. Nobody pays attention to me. Nobody will even take a meeting with me. I've tried everything. What do you suggest?"

After giving it a lot of thought, I came to only one conclusion, that Frank had to stop being like everyone else, and start being his authentic self. Because only then would he purposely attract the right kind of customer.

Here's what we did:

Step 1: Stop trying to compete with the faceless big brands with more than 100 years of experience. You're never going to win that meeting, Frank. You're just not. It's time to start creating your own brand image. The true authentic brand of Frank.

Step 2: To do this, you're going to create a blog where you're not going to talk about money or finances and the stock market. Instead, you're going to talk about the following things. 1. Your family. 2. Your political views. 3. Your religion. 4. Your take on the world. 5. Everything you believe in your core.

Yes, Frank, you're going to pick a tribe, your tribe, the one you already belong to, and you're going to double down on it.

"But Jim, everything I've been taught since I was a little boy was to not talk about my politics, or my religion. You want me to ignore that completely? That's scary."

Yes Frank, I do, and here's why. Because unless you want to wait 20 years to gain the trust of your target audience, you're going to need to find a quick way, and that is to share a common belief with them.

Here's the part of the story about Frank I haven't told you yet. Frank was very outspoken in his private life. He had very specific beliefs about politics, religion and world views that he shared with people in private, but never with social media, and certainly not with potential customers.

But that was his mistake, and we were going to correct it. We set up Frank's new blog and my instructions to him were simple: Let it all out. Do not hold back.

And that's what Frank did. He wrote scathing political pieces. He wrote long diatribes about his faith. He talked about his family and the values he embodied. And a lot of it was VERY inflammatory and outrageous.

But, it was authentic Frank. It was real.

As I watched Frank post, I even became a bit uncomfortable with what he was writing and saying as we share many opposite views. However, I knew that what he was doing was going to work. I knew that he was going to purposely attract the right customer.

About six months went by and I didn't hear from Frank until one day he invited me to lunch. As we sat down and ordered Frank told me something that I loved to hear.

He said, "Jim, just wanted to let you know that yesterday afternoon I signed on the biggest client I have ever had, times ten. He is going to let me handle his seven-figure retirement fund for him."

He continued. "And it's all because of my blog. I met my new client at a networking event right after I started the blog and gave him my blog address. This guy became my best friend almost overnight. He started commenting on every blog post. He started inviting me to golf with him and out to drinks and dinner. He's a great guy. We've become really good friends. And you know why? Because we share the same beliefs and values."

To summarize; Frank became his authentic self and proclaimed his views to his tribe. This caused another member of his tribe to be purposely attracted to him, thus earning him trust and eventually his business.

Do you think that Merrill Lynch could do this? Do you think they would try this? Not in your lifetime. Because they don't have to, yet. But as you will read further on in this book, there might come a day when they might not have any other choice.

Key Point: You become Unskippable not when you try to appeal to everyone, but when you purposely attract those who absolutely believe what your brand believes.

* * *

The Most Famous Ice Cream Brand In The World Chose A Tribe

If you're true to what you believe in, how can it go wrong?

According to USAToday, Ben & Jerry's is launching a new flavor called Pecan Resist, which the company made to promote activism in the U.S.

The Limited Batch flavor – chocolate ice cream with white and dark fudge chunks, pecans, walnuts and fudge-covered almonds – is part of the company's campaign to "lick injustice and champion those fighting to create a more just and equitable nation for us all."

Ben & Jerry's, which Unilever acquired in 2000, has used its sweet treats to promote its social justice agenda before. For example, Chubby Hubby became Hubby Hubby in 2009 to celebrate same sex marriage in Vermont, Chocolate Fudge Brownie was temporarily renamed Food Fight Fudge Brownie to support GMO labeling and EmpowerMint in 2016 was used to promote voting rights, the company said.

Do You Have To Choose A Controversial Tribe?

Frank did, and it worked, amazingly well in fact. Yeti did, unintentionally, and that worked. Nike did, intentionally, and wow did that work. Ben and Jerry's did it too.

But do you? I get it, you're scared of picking a tribe. Who wouldn't be? But you're fighting for your business life now, and maybe you're a few months away from closing up shop or you can't make payroll.

Or maybe you're just not getting anywhere with your marketing and you can't seem to close any new clients.

Maybe you're stuck in the middle and things are okay, but your competition is drinking your milkshake. Maybe you're not growing. Maybe you're losing market share.

It's amazing when I give this speech to an audience of real estate agents, or entrepreneurs, or tech startups, when they come up to me afterwards and tell me this is exactly where they are. They are struggling, and nothing they seem to do is moving the needle in the positive direction.

So, they go and buy more ads or rewrite their tagline, or

create more content marketing, when they should really be thinking about what their audience believes instead.

Do you need to choose a tribe? No. But then again, maybe you might just go out of business. It's your choice.

If you believe in something, truly believe, then what is the downside to not proclaiming that belief to customers who share it with you? A few bad social media comments? A national news story that sends your sales through the roof and changes everything for your business?

How horrible that would be. That's sarcasm.

There are those that believe we're living in a time of another eventual civil war. That the divide between the tribes will reach a boiling point and violence will become the next step in the battle for who is right and who is wrong.

It can be argued, in some ways, that this is already occurring in small batches. In any society that includes tribes there will always be extremism by some of the members of each tribe.

Currently, what we have is tribes who are battling out on social media through a war of words/videos/podcast/media, etc. But we also have extremists who cowardly take the battle further into the realm of personal harm beyond just thoughts and expression of ideas.

But what happens when the battle of words on social media isn't enough for the majority of the tribe? What happens when the "win" has to be more than just winning an argument?

I'll ask you again. Put your business hat on. Take the emotion out of it.

Would you rather have 1 percent of the entire market, or 100 percent of half of it?

Would choosing a tribe and doubling down on it have a chance of turning things around for you? Would taking a stance endear you to your belief-driven buyers and change everything for you?

These are legitimate questions you need to consider, and eventually answer. The future of your business may depend on it.

What happens when your biggest, or weakest, competitor does it before you? Where will you be then? Are you the leader of your pack, or the follower?

Labels suck and you have been taught that labeling your brand to one side or the other is a big no-no. It goes against all instincts. But that's the world we're now living in.

You like Nike? You must be a liberal idiot. You are an NRA member? You must be a right-wing nut. There isn't even the slightest possibility in a person's mind that neither of those statements are true, depending on which tribe you subscribe to. And that's a huge problem.

But it's also just the reality. So, as a business owner, or entrepreneur, you've got to understand this is where we're at, and what we've become, and figure out how the heck you're going to survive.

In 1996 when Roger Ailes was hired to run the upstart Fox News Network the very first thing he did was ask his fellow employees, "Who is our audience?" The story goes that they responded, "We want to reach everyone; the widest net possible."

Wrong answer. Ailes understood that to stand out, he needed to create a channel targeted at one tribe. In other words, the "half" of the 100 percent. Almost immediately Fox News became the choice for half of the country, quickly catapulting it to one of the most watched, and most profitable news organizations in the world.

In 2016 Fox News generated $1.6 billion in profits according to Deadspin.com. All from picking a tribe.

Since that time the other networks realized the same thing and created counter programming for their tribe, against Fox News, only to see their ratings and profits skyrocket as well. Meanwhile, news organizations in the middle who refused to pick a tribe continue to flounder in the ratings, and in profits.

Take your emotion out of it. You may love Fox News, or you may really despise it. It doesn't matter what your personal feelings are on it. The reality is we may be a tribal country/world, but we are also still a consumer based one.

The thing is before, and more so now: it's all intersecting.

This is politics come to life in everyday life now performed by every citizen. We're all running our own big campaign on social media for our beliefs, whether that's about politics, religion, the environment or any other "hot button" issue.

And the scary part is, all it's doing is dividing us and making us weaker.

The question for you is, are you going to capitalize on it, or not? That's such a horrible thing to say and consider. But let's be honest, this is where we're at.

Look at Nike. They chose a side. They figured out who their tribe was and pandered to it like a politician would.

The stakes are sky-high. There is no more reason and consideration. You are either a friend or an enemy. We exist in a living, breathing civil war of opinions and warring tribes who have zero consideration for whom they are at war with, and no plans to listen, only destroy and punish, or as I like to put it Ban, Blame, Boycott and Shame (BBBS).

When did we change? We can pinpoint this change in humanity to the cultural embrace of social media, for sure. This was the moment when the world got their voice and a medium to share it.

But the real tipping point, in my opinion, seemed to come around 2015 as our political landscape and divisiveness escalated to an entirely new level. How did we get there?

There has always been discourse accompanied with unrest, throughout human history. In the United States, The Civil War was perpetuated by two tribes of people (North vs. South) that had opposing views on a major issue. We all know what happened there. Hundreds of thousands of citizens lost their lives in a fight for what they believed in.

But today is different. Now global citizens choose to not pick up guns and shoot each other, but instead fight the war online, sometimes against their friends, family and associates.

And yes, the fight continues with who they do business with

and who they recommend. That's why it's more important than ever to understand how you as a business owner approach your political views and opinions, and how you decide to express what you believe in.

* * *

The Consumer Mindset: When Did Winning Become Everything?

Me: The sky is blue!

You: No, it's not, it's red!

Me: Oh really? How dare you tell me my truth is wrong.

You: I'm offended! Now I must destroy you.

In tribal warfare, there are no degrees of tribal loyalty. You're either on one side, or the other. There is no in between. You're either with us, or against us. There is no middle.

Your customers want you to choose, and heaven forbid you make a mistake and offend someone by accident (or on purpose), you can end up watching part of your customer base (and even those who aren't already) try to burn your business/brand to the ground.

Politics has become life. Future elections and purchases aren't about issues anymore. They're about which tribe you are in, and how your tribe can increase its power. This is the new brand loyalty.

We are all now in it for a win - just like a politician.

Everyone must win. Win every argument. Win everything, at all costs.

Note: Of course not everybody is like this. I'm speaking in general terms. You quite possibly aren't like this at all. However, that doesn't change the fact that a LOT of people are like this and you need to understand how they think, before you can sell something to them.

A reporter says something you believe is wrong? A win is getting them fired.

A business owner decides to do something you don't agree with? A win is destroying that business, not just forgoing buying from them going forward.

No, they must be destroyed, and any person who disagrees with you needs to be destroyed with them. It's insidious and ridiculous all at the same, but it is the reality of what we face in today's world.

A business owner needs to understand this in order to navigate it, if they can.

Social media has given megaphones to crowds, which creates constant mobile inflammation - and all behind the wall of anonymity. It's viral and accepted, to an extent.

Our tribes lift us up on their shoulders when we proclaim the same beliefs, which, in turn creates trust between them and us. And trust creates influence and power, which leads to, you guessed it, consumerism triggered by beliefs.

This wasn't always the case; all this vitriol. Politicians I know that have worked as civil servants for decades say it never used to be this way. For the most part, they say, in the past, that you fought your political opponent, but at the end of the day you'd go and have a beer after.

It's different now. Your tribe is not only part of your life campaign, they're living it with you, which makes them complicit in your success or failure, which in turn makes them more aggressive than they ever have been.

Is this a good thing? Probably not. Is the fact that people have more of a voice and are technically more educated now than ever before a detriment or asset to our way of life?

Who can answer that? History, I suppose.

But again, let's stop trying to answer those difficult questions, and start understanding instead.

You can never truly have success with your business, life or career until you start understanding your customer.

When I ran for office and met with and sat down with thousands of my constituents, I finally began to understand what they really wanted, and what they believed in.

Don't you find it interesting that someone might put a sign for a politician in their yard without thought, but if you asked them to put a sign promoting your potato chips or toothpaste, they'd think you were crazy?

Well that's actually changing. Tribalism is part of it, sure. But in today's world, when you find a brand that you love, or that you hate, you are MORE than willing to put up your very own virtual yard sign on social media telling the rest of the world about it.

In 2018 Jonathan Haidt and Greg Lukianoff co-authored

The Coddling of the American Mind. The book is an analysis of the toxic atmosphere in which our current debates take place, a reminder that it is close to impossible, in this polarized climate, to deal with the specifics and complexities of each scandal from a non-tribal perspective.

These two are no slouches. They know what they're talking about. From their Amazon bios.

Greg Lukianoff is the president and CEO of the Foundation for Individual Rights in Education (FIRE). Lukianoff is a graduate of American University and Stanford Law School. He specializes in free speech and First Amendment issues in higher education.

Jonathan Haidt is the Thomas Cooley Professor of Ethical Leadership at New York University's Stern School of Business. He obtained his Ph.D. in social psychology from the University of Pennsylvania in 1992, and then taught at the University of Virginia for 16 years.

Haidt and Lukianoff say that humans are constructed genetically for tribal warfare. That we divide the world instinctively into in-groups and out-groups almost from infancy.

Now add social media to the mix and your small backyard bonfire just turned into a chemical plant fire in Omaha, broadcast on Facebook live with comments and judgements.

The mobs and tribes have always been here. What Haidt and Lukianoff argue is some understanding on why they have grown into something so big and uncontrollable.

One argument is that if you were to give anonymity to a

mob, their capacity for violent and aggressive conduct suddenly soars.

Again, understanding is our goal.

This is where you need to be. Stop being emotional about your customer and instead start understanding why they think the way they do. Then, and only then, can you start your journey to becoming Unskippable.

If you've gotten this far into the book I'm confident you are enjoying it. Which is why I'm also confident that you are open to the ideas/concepts that I've been presenting.

Congratulations, you win for still being here!

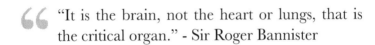 "It is the brain, not the heart or lungs, that is the critical organ." - Sir Roger Bannister

PART III: HOW TO BECOME UNSKIPPABLE

*A*lright, in the first two parts of this book we talked about what it means to be Unskippable, and also how to understand how people think, react and buy in today's complex world.

Now let's jump into some more ideas about how you can become Unskippable in your own business, life or career.

* * *

How A $400,000 Piano Changed The Music World Forever, Or Did It?

In 1975 a young man with the given name of Farrokh Bulsara conceived a song in his head that would eventually become one of the greatest and most well known songs in music history. The piece was over six minutes long, and included several sections including an introduction, a ballad segment, an operative passage, a hard rock part and finally a reflective coda.

When the song was first introduced to the media it was lauded as garbage with reviews such as, "a superficially impressive pastiche of incongruous musical styles" and "It has no immediate selling point whatsoever: among its many parts. There's scarcely a shred of a tune and certainly no one line to latch onto."

Time magazine called it, "pretentious and irrelevant."

The song? *Bohemian Rhapsody*. The artist? Queen & Freddy Mercury.

Here's another fun fact. The piano that Mercury used to record *Bohemian Rhapsody* is also the same one that Paul McCartney and The Beatles used to record *Hey Jude* seven years earlier. Of course, *Hey Jude* was another transformational song that is also one of the most popular and memorable pieces of music the modern world has ever seen.

It gets better. David Bowie's *"Space Oddity"* and George Harrison's solo album *"All Things Must Pass"* (among others) were also recorded using the century-old Bechstein Grand Piano, which currently resides in London at Trident Studios and is currently valued at $400,000.

That's some piano. Oh, the stories it could tell!

But here's the thing. It's just a piano.

Those songs and albums that changed the world that were recorded on it did not break through because of the piano.

They broke through because the people who wrote and performed the songs were Unskippable.

You see, at the time radio airplay determined if your song became popular, or not. Those that controlled the industry said that a song had to be under three minutes and meet the basic conventions of radio airplay.

Specifically, *Bohemian Rhapsody* was 5:55 long and *Hey Jude* came in at a whopping 7:11 thanks to a lot of "na, na, na, na's." In *Bohemian Rhapsody's* case, radio personalities didn't want to play it because of the length and because it was so different. The Beatles, well, they were the Beatles and that didn't matter, everyone played The Beatles.

What made those songs, and those albums, Unskippable was that the creators didn't care about the rules. They cared about the content. They cared about their vision.

True artists, the ones that change the world, take this approach at all costs.

But you're not an artist. You're a real estate agent from San Bernardino. Or you're an IT professional from Alaska. You're in business. You don't sell art.

Really? Ok, well, be prepared to be like everyone else you're competing with every single day then. Because having success, being Unskippable, is about breaking the mold and defying conventions and standing out and taking chances.

Or, you could just continue what you're doing with your marketing and your offerings and hope that you get that radio airplay. It's up to you.

Stop focusing on the tools. You don't need a $400,000 piano.

You need to change your mindset and start creating new

marketing and new ideas and new branding that sets you apart.

* * *

Unskippable People Are Happy Because They Foster New Friendships (Not On Facebook)

The average American hasn't made a new (real, not Facebook) friend in five years, according to a study conducted by OnePoll in collaboration with Evite.

Five years! So sad. The emergence of social media "friends" has widened our circles so far that we have essentially replaced "real" friendships with too many virtual friends.

To put it another way, we used to have to work to find friends, real ones, but now social media has given us too many, and because of that we're not looking for, or fostering the real friends we already have as much as we should.

"Not only are we not having intimate friends or relationships anymore, but kids that are in their twenties are not even having sex as much. It's the lack of connection anymore, this lack of intimacy that social media has created that people don't even know how to have sex anymore. It's scary," says JB Glossinger, the Morning Coach, who's a Ph.D in Metaphysics and has been motivating people for over 15-years through his daily CoachCast podcast with over 3,500 episodes and 26 million downloads.

This is a big problem for all of us. Why? Because real friendships are what really make us happy, even though most people think it's money and fame.

Robert Waldinger, a psychiatrist from the Harvard School of Adult Development, did a TED talk where he offers the results of 75 years of studying happiness.

For three-quarters of a century they studied people over their lifetimes and came to one big conclusion. "The clearest message that we get from this 75-year study is this. Good relationships keep us happier and healthier," says Waldinger.

Glossinger agrees 100 percent. "One of my biggest things and biggest successes over the last couple years has been the masterminds that I put together and getting together with real people," he says.

"I mean that literally the community is more important than anything else I think I've ever created and I'm learning that more and more. I'm learning that from a business perspective that I needed to have more boots on the street.

It's getting tougher and tougher to convert people from social media or even coaching systems via the Internet. It's more important that I speak and then I talk to real people and I connect with real people. That's what works for me now.

Comparatively, 10 years ago it was so easy to just create a landing page and buy some Facebook ads to convert. All that's changing, all of it's changing.

And I really think the reason is because people are getting tired of all that noise and you've got to be able to connect one-on-one. You've got to be able to connect in a real life."

Like you, maybe, I've been on the cusp of deleting my

social media accounts. I don't feel social media is enhancing my life more than it is potentially causing issues with it.

I've been culling my "friends" to only people that I want to hear from, and proactively keeping an eye on those "friends" to make sure they're not being negative, or arguing about politics, or whatever else that bothers me.

Maybe this is just where my head is at the time of my life and writing this book, but I am constantly asking myself questions like, "How do I want to spend the rest of my life?

Do I want to spend it being negative and complaining about things on Facebook, or do I want to be the best version of myself where I put my time and energy into my family and real friendships?"

Perhaps you've asked yourself those same questions?

Back to the study from Waldinger's talk. He said that they learned three big lessons about relationships.

#1 Lesson - Social connections are really good for us, and loneliness kills.

"It turns out that people who are more socially connected to family, to friends, to community, are happier, they're physically healthier, and they live longer than people who are less well connected. And the experience of loneliness turns out to be toxic.

People who are more isolated than they want to be from others find that they are less happy, their health declines earlier in midlife, their brain functioning declines sooner and they live shorter lives than people who are not lonely. And the sad fact is that at any given time, more than one in five Americans will report that they're lonely."

Again, have you given yourself the illusion that you're not

lonely because you have 500 Facebook friends and 1,230 Twitter followers? Because those aren't "real" friends.

The faux happiness you might be feeling from social media connections might be the toxicity that is making you less happy and declining your health. And you might not even realize it.

#2 Lesson - It's not just the number of friends you have, and it's not whether or not you're in a committed relationship, but it's the quality of your close relationships that matters.

"It turns out that living in the midst of conflict is really bad for our health. High-conflict marriages, for example, without much affection, turn out to be very bad for our health, perhaps worse than getting divorced. And living in the midst of good, warm relationships is protective.

Once we had followed our men all the way into their 80s, we wanted to look back at them at midlife and to see if we could predict who was going to grow into a happy, healthy octogenarian and who wasn't.

And when we gathered together everything we knew about them at age 50, it wasn't their middle age cholesterol levels that predicted how they were going to grow old. It was how satisfied they were in their relationships.

The people who were the most satisfied in their relationships at age 50 were the healthiest at age 80. And good, close relationships seem to buffer us from some of the slings and arrows of getting old.

Our most happily partnered men and women reported, in their 80s, that on the days when they had more physical pain, their mood stayed just as happy. But the people who were in unhappy relationships, on the days when they reported more physical pain, it was magnified by more emotional pain."

When you're 80 years-old are your social media friends going to bring you comfort? Or will it be your spouse, or other close personal "real" relationships that will help you live happier?

#3 Lesson - Good relationships don't just protect our bodies, they protect our brains.

"It turns out that being in a securely attached relationship to another person in your 80s is protective, that the people who are in relationships where they really feel they can count on the other person in times of need, those people's memories stay sharper longer.

And the people in relationships where they feel they really can't count on the other one, those are the people who experience earlier memory decline. And those good relationships, they don't have to be smooth all the time.

Some of our octogenarian couples could bicker with each other day in and day out, but as long as they felt that they could really count on the other when the going got tough, those arguments didn't take a toll on their memories."

Can you count on your Twitter followers? Of course not.

Look, relationships are messy. Real ones outside of social media, especially. Waldinger said that, "The people in our 75-year study who were the happiest in retirement were the people who had actively worked to replace workmates with new playmates." And, "Over and over, over these 75 years, our study has shown that the people who fared the best were the people who leaned in to relationships, with family, with friends, with community."

If you want to become Unskippable in your own happiness, it might be time to start thinking about your current relationships, and taking some action to ensure you don't end up on your deathbed a lonely, bitter fool.

But how?

Maybe end a grudge with a family member that has kept you apart. Maybe start replacing your video game or Netflix watching time with actually meeting with or talking to a true friend.

Maybe, just maybe, stop valuing your social media connections as real relationships and start focusing on those people right in front of your face, in your everyday "real" life.

It's funny, when the Internet started it was an escape from the real world. But things have changed. Now the real world is an escape from the Internet in ways.

* * *

Unskippable Brands Don't Focus On Benefits, They Focus On Emotions

Speaking of real friendships. Real friends help you experience joy through emotional connections. And so do Unskippable brands.

People don't buy an $800 pair of shoes on "reason", they do it on emotion. This is an older stat, but Forbes.com says that, "American women spent nearly $17 billion on fashion footwear between October 2004 and October 2005."

$17 billion? Wow! Why?

"Shoes make women feel so beautiful that they're willing to pay anything," says Jessie Randall, the Brooklyn, N.Y.-based designer and founder of Loeffler Randall, a shoe and handbag line she founded with her husband. "You can't put a price on something that makes you feel that special."

Emotions create reactions. Our societal obsession with consumption of "stuff that makes us feel good" is nothing new.

A belief-driven buyer makes a purchasing decision on emotion. Voters choose politicians based on emotion, not reason. Your boss probably decided to grant you that raise due to emotion, not reason.

The next person to Tweet something nice (or not nice) about you is absolutely doing so because of an emotional reaction to your product or service.

Gallup reported that nearly 80 percent of our country believes religion is losing its influence. As the numbers of followers of organized religions continue to dwindle, the question has been asked by many, are brands becoming a new religion?

Take a deep breath, I'm not going to start comparing Steve Jobs and Apple to Christianity. However, I will tell you that the connections and concepts of organized religion and successful brands are more common than you think, and understanding this is key to understanding how to create an Unskippable brand.

Think about it. Throw out the faith argument, and just focus on the commonalities. Both Unskippable brands and religions have loyal customer bases. They both, usually, have a strong driving principle that governs their mission.

They both, sometimes, have a visionary or charismatic leader.

Other common characteristics include community and value and positioning and loyalty - all things an Unskippable brand, or religion must have.

Believe it or not, there was a study done on this. In *Brands: The Opiate of the Nonreligious Masses?*, a paper published in *Marketing Science*, it is theorized that those who feel strongly about favored brands, known as brand reliance, would exhibit less engagement with religion, or religiosity, and vice versa.

In other words, as more and more people are choosing to not follow religion, they are turning to brands instead.

Blasphemy! I know, this kind of stuff can really hurt if you believe it because it challenges our belief structures. But the facts remain, humans want to believe in something, and if they don't believe in religion, they're turning to brands to fill that void, sometimes.

What it comes down to is self worth. From the study, "Brands and religiosity serve as substitutes for one another because both allow individuals to express their feelings of self worth. Brands have evolved over the last hundred years, and they've become more central to our sense of self. They're our way to signal to others who we are. Brands provide a sense of community. Even when we're alone, we have our brand community to feel a part of."

Stop for a moment. I want you to think about your business. What community type feeling have you fostered with your customers?

I've never owned a Jeep, but I've always been fascinated about why Jeep owners wave at each other when they drive by each other.

Yeah, it's a real thing, and it's called "The Jeep Wave Club" and it's an exclusive group ONLY for Jeep owners. Who started it? The Internet isn't sure, but it's real.

This is how it is described on hundreds of websites. "The Jeep Wave is an honor bestowed upon those drivers with the superior intelligence, taste, class and discomfort tolerance to own the ultimate vehicle: The Jeep."

Essentially, here are the rules. Rule #1: If you see another Jeep on the road, you're supposed to wave. There are many styles of how you can do the Jeep wave. You're fine just giving a hearty, side-to-side wave above the windshield if you have the top off. You can also go for a more subtle wave with your thumb, index, and pointer fingers extended. What really matters is that you just wave.

Rule #2: Whomever has the newest Jeep waves first. There's even a point system you can apply for how many points you get for having the oldest Jeep. I'm not kidding.

Then, if you dig even deeper, you will find that this religion, um, I mean brand, has class systems and levels of believers and non-believers.

You see, there are the newbie Jeep owners who bought a Jeep just because they liked it as a type of SUV, not as "real" Jeep fans, and those people don't really get it so they don't know to wave. Then there are extremist Jeep owners who look down on anyone who doesn't modify or "supe up" their Jeep so they hold back their waves to the posers.

There is also a group of believers that won't offer a wave if your Jeep isn't covered in mud. There's even a Jeep Wave Calculator so if you want to tally up your personal points I guess you could do so.

I've always liked Jeeps, however, I've never owned one even though I've known about the wave for a long time. But I can honestly say that after researching this more in depth that I feel like I want to be part of that cult, I mean, club.

I want to belong. I want to give the wave. That's powerful psychological stuff.

By the way, if you own a motorcycle you have also experienced this wave system, and it's even more complex with many more levels of class hierarchies. Harley Davidson riders typically only wave to other Harley riders, and usually never to riders of foreign-made bikes.

When I asked my friend, who is a lifelong motorcycle rider, about why he does the wave he said, "It's the brotherhood thing which others won't feel if they aren't riding. Riding bikes is fun, and we tend to like to wave at each other to say, "Hey. You're not alone out here. You're part of the cool tribe."

Now back to you and your brand. What is your Jeep wave?

Could it be something as small as a bumper sticker? In Cleveland we have a chocolate factory called Malley's. Malley's followers put "CHOC" stickers on their cars to support the brand. The deal is if one of their employees spots the sticker on your car during a promotion, you get some free chocolate.

Now, call me crazy, but I'm not putting a permanent bumper sticker on my vehicle for the potential of a box of chocolate covered pretzels. But I'm the outlier because thousands and thousands of other people do.

That's building an Unskippable brand.

When I worked at a print shop in college the owner, Vern, used to put a handful of Jolly Ranchers in EVERY pickup. Ordered 100 business cards? You got Jolly Ranchers. Ordered 10,000 flyers? You got Jolly Ranchers. It was such a small, silly thing I thought at the time.

Until 25 years later when I ran into a former customer of Vern's and as we were reminiscing he said to me, "You know what I remember about Vern? It was those Jolly Ranchers he put in every order I got from him. I loved getting those."

It wasn't about how great Vern's business card printing was, it was about candy.

Vern was Unskippable, 25 years later. Do you remember who you bought business cards from 25 years ago?

That's how you build an Unskippable brand; even the littlest of things.

These examples all seem so trivial and small, but are they? When you understand that people want to belong, and that people want to be part of something, then you can start your journey to loyal, lifetime customers.

Unskippable People Are Unskippable Because?

If you want people to know, like and trust you so you can have a better career, or live a happier life, or start a successful business, there are a litany of things you can do to be your best self.

You don't have to be perfect, or do everything, to accomplish that goal. But you do have to have an understanding of what people are attracted to and have the proper mindset to move forward.

Here's a lightning round of examples that you can apply to your life goals in whatever career or business you are in.

Unskippable People Ship, Skippable People Perfect

You can spend your entire life attempting to write the next great American novel, but at some point, you have to put it out into the world. My author friend J. Thorn released his first Horror book on Amazon years ago without a professional edit and no advance readers.

Guess what? It was a complete disaster. He got tons of one-star reviews and barely sold any copies. Fast forward to almost 10 years later.

Because he "shipped" his book into the universe, he was able to learn what not to do. He removed that first book and went back and fixed his mistakes and wrote more books. Since then, he has amassed over three million words written across 15 new books, created his own publishing company and quit his day job to live his dream of being a full-time author.

This is a bitter pill to swallow for perfectionists, I get it.

Perhaps you might not be able to mentally overcome the idea that everything is not going to be perfect. But the fact remains that until you ship your product out the door, you have NO IDEA how people are going to respond to it, and you're never going to learn anything from not failing.

Unskippable People Overdeliver, Skippable People Do "Just Enough"

Not getting the pay raise you believe you deserve? If only your boss would just notice you. I'm not going to accuse you specifically of not being the best employee your office ever had, but I will, in a general sense, say that most people want to do just enough, and that's why they never move up the ladder.

If you like your job and you do want that pay raise, then maybe the better plan is to start over-delivering on expectations.

Imagine what the boss thinks when they arrive every morning to see your car there first, before them? Imagine what the owner thinks when you take the initiative to work on a new product or service that could make the company more money?

On the flip side, imagine what the boss thinks when they see that you're leaving 15 minutes early every other day? Imagine what the owner thinks when they see you just doing the bare minimum to get by?

Remember, doing an adequate job isn't going to get you noticed in a good way.

To get noticed in today's world, you have to exceed expectations.

* * *

Unskippable People Let Go Of Grudges & Move On

I wasn't kidding about that grudge I held after losing my election. I was angry, really angry when I lost. I had basically given two years of my life, at the expense of my business, my marriage and my kids, to try and make my town a better place.

And then the people I worked so hard for basically said to me, "You suck." It hurt. I was angry at them, the voters. Then I was even more angry at the opponents that attacked me and told lies about me. It was just so personal to me.

So, for a year I festered with it, and pouted about it. I couldn't seem to let it go until one day I realized it was over, and I was not going to be able to move on with my life until I did.

If you're one of those people who voted me out of office, or if you're one of my political opponents who told lies about me, I forgive you. I'm over it. The grudge is gone and I've moved on.

Once I moved on things started to change for me in a really positive way. I learned so much about people, the good, and the bad during my dark political days.

I ended up getting a better understanding of who I was and what was really important to me and how I wanted to live out the rest of my life. And that thought process really shaped this book. So, in a way I'm grateful for the experience, as bad as it was.

That's the thing. I'm the type of person that learns from the negative stuff, then takes it and adjusts to it and puts a positive spin on it. I know others that take the opposite approach and stay down on themselves and walk around saying the world is out to get them and continue with the negativity.

You gotta stop that crap. It's taking you NOWHERE.

Like JB Glossinger says, "It's a poison. Anything that's kind of negative like that is really poison that just eats at you and you have to learn to let go."

Here's my challenge to you. Do what I did and make a promise that you are not going to post anything negative on social media ever again. You're only going to post positive things.

You're not going to complain about anything. Not the long line when getting your new driver's license. Not the ending of some TV show you were disappointed in. Nothing. You're only going to share or comment on positive things in your life or others.

I made this pledge years ago and I've stuck to it. I can honestly tell you it has changed me for the better. The next step is just getting rid of social media all together. I'm not there yet, but soon, very soon.

Unskippable People/Business Tell Powerful Stories

Chubbies is an online retailer that sells shorts and swim trunks. But what then they talk about what they do, they say, "We sell weekends". They don't say, "We sell shorts".

Weekends are fun. We look forward to weekends. Shorts are just shorts. We don't look forward to shorts.

What do you do? How do you say what you do? Can you say it in 10 words or less? Can you say it quickly enough?

Because remember people want to skip you.

The concept of the elevator pitch is so cliche. You know what it is. An elevator ride is typically about 30 seconds or less. If you had to tell your story to someone in that ride, you better be able to do it concisely and quickly.

However cliche it is, it's still a good lesson for all of us, and a good pitch or story definitely makes you more Unskippable.

If you do not know, the elevator pitch came about because, well, I've heard a bunch of different stories. On Wikipedia they source at least five origin stories. I'm just gonna go with the best, most fun one first. It goes like this.

Elisha Graves Otis was the inventor of a device meant for elevator safety. This was back in 1852, back when the safety concept of these new things called elevators was probably like convincing someone to jump off a tall building. How do you get people to believe that it's safe?

Well, Otis gathered the press into a warehouse and stood on top of an elevator equipped with his safety device. He raised the elevator to dangerous height and then cut the rope that held the elevator in place. Yes, early elevators used ropes, not cables.

When the rope was cut, Otis's safety device was enabled

and he didn't die. He then gave a speech. Not dying is Unskippable. Nice work Otis!

But this story is probably more true. A guy by the name of Philip Crosby was working as a quality test technician for International Telephone and Telegraph. He wanted to see changes in how the company did business, so he planned a speech and he waited at the elevator in the company head-quarters until the CEO of the company got in.

Once inside with the CEO, he gave his speech. 30 seconds later, the CEO invited Crosby to deliver a full presentation on his idea to the entire company.

When I speak to entrepreneur groups I tell them this. "I teach entrepreneurs how to fire their boss, forever." In those nine words I have communicated what I do that helps them and that is way more effective than a paragraph of (boring) descriptive content that they probably aren't going to read anyway.

When I pitch you about this book, or event bookers to speak at their events I say, "I inspire the uninspired to create a better business, life or career."

So again, what do you say when someone asks you what you do?

Let's break it down so it's easier to understand and you can apply it to yourself or your business. Here's the basic formula. You can work it around for your own purpose, but this is basically how it should go.

"I/We" + *"Do Something"* + *"For This Specific Person/Group"* + *"Achieve A Specific Result".*

Example: I help homeowners save thousands on their yearly taxes.

Example: We teach small business owners how to grow their business using social media.

Avoid jargon and industry words. Those just get you into trouble. Is what you wrote good enough to explain it to a child? And for the love of God, don't say "we're making the world a better place".

Stop reading this book for a second. Go write your pitch. Try to keep it 10 words or less, if you can. Then come back.

Startups are really bad at this stuff. An article on Quartz.com entitled *Startups can't explain what they do because they're addicted to meaningless jargon,* the author points to a company named Undone, which is a Hong Kong startup that makes custom-designed watches.

They describe themselves as a "disruptive consumer brand with state of the art customization technology with original content platform."

I've got news for you guys at Undone, you make watches, plain and simple. Are they cool? Yeah, probably. Are they "disruptive?" Probably not.

It's a watch, bro.

Imagine running into the CEO of this company at a party and asking him what they do and he comes back with that line of you know what?

You don't want to do that in person, and you don't want to do that in a meeting with a potential investor or customer.

* * *

Unskippable Brands Get Married To Their Customers

What is the main mission of marketing? Most people would say it is to "attract new customers". And they'd be right. But here's a better way of thinking about it.

Marketing's main mission is to: **PURPOSELY** attract **LIFETIME** customers.

Two key words have been added: Purposely & Lifetime.

The purposely part we all get. It's another way of saying you should market to a specific audience, or targeted customer. Hopefully you're already doing that. But how do you take it a step further?

In the previous pages of this book you could decide to "purposely" try and attract a specific belief-driven buyer, and it might work really well.

But the addition of the word lifetime is really the big mindset change you need to make when you are trying to become Unskippable.

A lifetime customer is the holy grail we should all be on a quest for. A lifetime customer means you spend less on advertising because your customer does it for you.

A lifetime customer is your life partner.

Remember, the consumer has changed. They no longer want "just a product", or "just a service." They want to get married and buy a house in the suburbs and have 2.5 kids with your brand. Through thick and thin, until death do you part.

You want that lifetime marriage and that commitment just as much as they do, probably more. So "purposely" attract a "lifetime" partner, and put a ring on it!

* * *

Unskippable Marketing Is Human, Not Automated

Let's remove the word funnel from our vocabulary, okay?

We've reached a tipping point in our marketing and that bubble is about to burst. In our never-ending quest for the ultimate conversion rate we have forgotten that what really brings lifetime, loyal customers is value and meaning in what we do and what we represent. Not chatbots, or content marketing, or sales funnels, or split-testing.

Somewhere along the way our wires got crossed about the way we need to communicate to, and with, our potential customers. Most businesses today have sipped the Kool-Aid and focus on getting attention, then go straight to conversion, leaving the most important part of the equation, value, lost in space.

I follow a lot of Internet marketers and I see way too many conversations like:

Should I be focusing on chatbots or messenger ads?

Here's how I increased my sales funnel success from 3 percent open rates to 300 percent!

This simple headline trick will get more people to click on your blog posts.

Ugh.

How do you market effectively in 2019 and beyond? You get rid of all that stuff and start focusing on connecting with people one-to-one, as a human.

* * *

Unskippable People/Businesses Create Moments Of Epiphany To Create True Fans

True fans are true believers, but they don't turn into that by means of your typical sales and marketing messages. My point is, you don't become a disciple of anything after reading some sales copy - that's just not enough.

It takes time and a really good, convincing argument to win someone over. Let's talk about how to convince someone to become a true believer in you, or your business.

You can throw out the best content marketing you can think of. You can create the best viral video that's ever been done. You can keep pushing traditional benefit-based marketing tactics. And you can hope they work, and they might. But to truly convince someone into following you into the afterlife, you have to find a way to let them come to that conclusion on their own.

In other words, they have to find a way for them to have an epiphany on their own. How?

Persuasion, and negotiation.

All that great content marketing we keep producing is great at talking "to" your audience, but it isn't so great at talking "with" them.

A negotiation is a form of persuasion, that when mastered, will create a disciple. We negotiate with ourselves and the people around us all day, every day. We do it with our friends and coworkers. We do it with our significant others.

Here are some ideas on how to better negotiate with yourself, and everyone else in your life.

* * *

Unskippable People/Businesses Understand Their Customer's Pain

You know what you want. You probably also understand what your customer wants. But do you understand why they want it? What pain do they have that is causing them to want to negotiate with you?

Forget about price negotiations from people who just want to pay less even though they have the money. What I'm talking about is other types of negotiations like marital compromises, or dealing with an unruly child or a business deal.

Why do they want to negotiate? What's their pain point?

Until you understand that, you're just playing chicken.

Ask them why they aren't willing to take the deal as is and then clear the objections. Could it be that they just don't have enough money? Probably. Once you find that out, are you willing to drop your price to get the sale?

Unless you're selling a physical product with small margins, what's the downside to lowering the price to something they can afford as a compromise?

Maybe, just maybe, they'll be grateful to you and leave you a nice review, or share it with their friends? Oh, and you still got paid something. That's more revenue than you had before!

Could it be that they want to feel power over you? Children rebel because they are flexing their muscles and want to be in control instead of the other way around. Give your child some power then.

They don't want to eat that broccoli? Fine, but they have to decide what vegetable they DO want to eat. I'll let you choose, you have the power now.

The LAST thing you should do is belittle their why. That's when a negotiation ends, and war starts.

Unskippable People/Businesses Persuade By Giving Control Away

As in the example above about the child not wanting to eat his broccoli, you are giving control away, not trying to hold onto it.

Dell is famous for this. Before Dell, if you wanted a PC you went to the store and bought one, as is. Dell changed the game by giving the control to you do build what you want instead. Want a bigger hard drive and a CD-ROM- and more memory? Okay, YOU choose that.

All of a sudden the power goes to the consumer and it's no

longer "Do you want to buy this PC?" to "What kind of PC do you want and what should it look like and what should be in it?" That's a much different conversation.

You walk into your boss's office say, "I want a raise and a promotion." She says, "No, go back to work." Maybe a better approach is, "I'm having a hard time financially at my current salary (that's your why). What kind of employee do I need to be to qualify for more money and what do you think I need to do to show that I am ready for a promotion?"

Interested in more about persuasion? If you have never read Dr. Cialdini's amazing book *Influence*, you should. You don't have to be a marketer to apply his lessons to every part of your life.

Of course, before you go read his book, finish this one first!

Unskippable People Start Becoming Successful When They Stop Doing Things They Hate

I hate doing social media for business purposes. I hate posting updates, writing blog posts, tweeting, and everything else. I do the bare minimum because I'm forced to for my business. But I really hate it.

I also hate doing the finances and my taxes. This is why I pay people to do all those things for me.

Think of how much you could get done by focusing on the things you love to do instead? The time and money you spend on the ones you hate will easily be made up from the work you do on what you love doing.

Unskippable People Do Unexpected, Generous Things For Others

Here's your challenge, should you choose to accept it. I want you to pick one person who is awesome in your life, and I want you to do something nice, or fun, or generous for them today. The rest of this book can wait.

Pick somebody right now. A family member, or high-school buddy, or co-worker or anybody who is just a nice person and you like. Your motive is simple. You want to show them how much you appreciate them, that's it.

Now, what do you know about that person? In conversations did they ever mention they love a certain band, or drink, or food or whatever? Not sure? Check their social media posts. Maybe they posted something you can find there.

Next, take 10-minutes and try to come up with something fun or unique you could give them, or help them with. Example: They love margaritas. Go to the store and buy some margarita mix and some tequila and show up at their house and give it to them.

Or just drop it off on their porch and text them to go get it. "I was thinking about you today when I was in the store and I remembered you love margaritas. I saw stuff to make them, so I just bought it for you. Enjoy!"

You don't have to spend a lot of money. In fact, you probably shouldn't. Just do something fun or silly or just meaningful for that person.

That's it. It's that simple. See how it feels. And when you realize how good it feels, do it again, and again.

By the way, you can also create more loyalty and trust in a customer by trying the same thing with your business.

When monitoring your social media have you ever come across a brand fan that can't stop gushing about you? Imagine how much more they would evangelize for you if you found their mailing address and sent them one of your products out of the blue as a thank you.

You can't pay for advertising that good, so why not foster it?

* * *

Utility Is What Makes You Unskippable, Not "Features".

Unskippable brands focus on making better products, not adding more features.

I was one of the very first adopters of the Flip video camera, which was very popular right before iPhones were released. A Flip camera was a simple video recording device that did one thing: record video. Then you "flipped" the little USB out of the side, connected it to your computer, and you had video.

I produced hundreds of videos on my little Flip camera back in the day, which I uploaded to sites like Vimeo and YouTube. I loved my Flip. I had two of them, one in orange and one in black and I took them wherever I went.

Why was the Flip camera so great? Because it did one thing, and did it well. Sure, they could have added other functionality to it, but then it would have been too complex.

When you make things complex you create confusion and reduce ease of use.

Unskippable companies do less, not more. This can be argued in terms of how you design your product or service, or even your marketing messages.

Are you trying to please everyone, or should you just be trying to please one person, your target consumer? You can't be everything to everyone.

There are going to be people who really dislike what you've done, and people who really like it. Focus on the people who really like it.

And also remember, when there are people who don't like it, you've done your job, because skippable companies don't elicit emotional reactions in people, Unskippable companies do.

* * *

Unskippable Businesses Don't Automate, They Double Down On Human Connections

Authenticity expressed through your future marketing is the key to guiding your customer through their journey to your buy button.

In other words, stop trying to interrupt your customer with ads. Stop trying to automate your sales funnel with chat bots. Stop automating, period! Your customer does not want to talk to your robot employee.

As Mark Schaefer brilliantly states in his book *Marketing Rebellion*, "The most human company wins." And he's right, and that's where we're at now. It is a drastic turn from where we were, which was marketers working so hard to find ways to automate everything. Automate customer service. Automate returns. Automate sales.

It made sense at the time. The more you automate, the more you could potentially make in profits from hiring less people and/or saving time on tasks that human beings could do.

But therein lies the problem. When you try to take the human factor out of the equation, you're left with a soulless, faceless, robotic brand that nobody wants to do business with.

Do you really want to do business with a company that has no story? Do you really think you're going to create a long-term relationship with a brand that can't even let you pick up the phone and talk to them?

I've seen this scenario happen too often, and it's going to keep happening. A successful company gets too big, too fast and instead of trying to add more real people into the equation, they start to do the opposite and remove them.

Instead of you being able to pick up the phone and get your problem solved or your question answered, you're sent into an endless loop of automated messages designed to wear you out and stop you from getting what you wanted.

How is that sustainable? When, if ever, have you had that type of interaction with a company and you felt great about it after?

The answer is never. Why do companies do it? Because some guru told them they could increase profits.

"Very small businesses have a huge advantage over big companies as we can be human and personal more than they can.... And we can charge more for it." - Mark Schaefer

Unskippable Companies Know When To Pivot, & Innovate

 "Sport, like all life, is about taking risks." - Sir Roger Bannister

Times change, consumers change. Do you, ever? Maybe you should consider it.

I was once called into a company in the medical industry to do some consulting. Their competitors were swallowing them whole, and it was only a matter of months before they were finished.

They wanted an outside perspective on why. I met with them for a full-day learning about what they do and who they sell to. I was introduced to their products and how they market them. Then I spent two days on my own analyzing their competition and comparing it to them.

A week later, I walked into the client's board room and gave a presentation to 10 executives and the president of the company. The problem was clear - they hadn't adapted to the marketplace. Not only in their product offerings, but in their marketing. I laid it all out for them for an hour with charts and examples.

Their president sat there with his arms crossed the entire time and didn't say a word. When I was finished he got up and walked out the room without a word. The rest of the employees congratulated me saying, "You nailed it. This is what we've been saying." They were excited and ready to change gears.

Their jobs were saved! I walked out of the office knowing I had hit a home run.

The next day I got a call from the president of the company who informed me that what I presented was, in his opinion, a waste of money. He told me that I didn't know what I was talking about and that he knew his product, and his customers, and I was all wrong.

Fortunately, I got paid ahead of time. Nine months later the company went out of business. Why? Because the president refused to see his weaknesses, and he refused to pivot, while his competitors feasted on him until they swallowed him whole.

Times change. Consumers change.

IKEA is a $44 billion company. I had no idea they were that big, did you? Regardless, when you're that big, you can't fail, right? Well, yes you can, if you don't keep an eye on global economic shifts and consumer habits.

To head off any potential competitor, and to take advantage of the shift in consumer behavior, IKEA is testing out the rental model on their products.

Here's the thing. Younger buyers like renting assets more than buying them, and just that fact alone, if it continues, could create a huge risk to their build-it-yourself model that has done so well for IKEA.

Obviously, the riskiest part of this pivot is that by offering rentals IKEA could hurt their current model as customers would then have a choice of renting over buying. But is it really a risk in today's global marketplace? I argue that providing choices in what, and how, you sell is a better mousetrap.

Blockbuster stuck to its guns and didn't get into the streaming business because they feared it would destroy its in-store rental business. They also rejected delivery because they felt they could control the customer if they were forced to come into their stores.

We all know what happened to them. Netflix embraced delivery and eventually pivoted to streaming and is now a $28 billion company.

Interesting side note, in 2000 Netflix came to Blockbuster and wanted to partner where they would run Blockbuster online. Blockbuster thought Netflix's business model was a niche business and turned them down.

Kodak was one of the biggest brands in the world, but filed for bankruptcy in 2012. What's amazing is in 1975 Kodak actually invented the first digital camera, but because it was filmless photography they decided to keep it quiet and not move to market on it because it would hurt the film market.

What do you think the CEO of Blackberry thought the day that the iPhone came out? Was it doom, or hubris that "people love their Blackberrys, I'm not worried." Oops.

In 2005 Myspace was given the chance to buy Facebook for

$75 million, but they turned it down because "people love their Myspace." Sears, who recently announced 166 more store closings, didn't pivot when brands like Walmart built supercenters in every major suburb nationwide because "We're Sears, and people know Sears."

Shall I keep going?

Macy's department stores were founded over 100-years ago. In 1980 Macy's got pitched an idea to start a cable television channel to sell their stuff, but Macy's KNEW that their customers didn't want that experience, they wanted a traditional store. QVC started shortly after.

Traditional publishing companies had every opportunity to develop online marketplaces to sell books way before Jeff Bezos started Amazon, but they liked their model of selling books to bookstores, instead of directly to the customer. They even had the idea of digital books first, but they KNEW that print books would always sell better than eBooks.

Sometimes you pivot unintentionally. Did you know Viagra wasn't created for, well, you know? The scientific name for the drug is actually called Sildenafil and it was originally tested as a treatment for high blood pressure.

But the early tests were just "meh" from the male participants for helping with blood pressure. However, when the study was over, the participants refused to give back the unused pills.

Why you say? Because the side effect was, well, you know.

So Pfizer started another test, but this time it was for erectile dysfunction. In 1998 they got permission from the FDA to sell Viagra to consumers, and 20 years-later, and a few billion dollars in sales, Viagra and Pfizer changed the lives of millions.

All from understanding and pivoting on their customer's feedback.

Innovating isn't easy, and extremely risky, but the companies that keep their heads on a swivel to today's changing consumer trends tend to survive. So, I'll ask you this question; what is changing in your space? It might be time to consider that and get ahead of it.

How do you know when to pivot though?

First, talk to your customers. No, don't send them an online survey. Get 100, or 1,000 of them in a room and ask them what they love, and hate, about what you provide.

Second, study your competition, daily, and pay attention to what they are doing. Third, run the numbers and come up with a strategic plan. Fourth, make it happen!

* * *

Unskippable Brands Stand Out From The Crowd, By Understanding What The Crowd Thinks

Whether you're writing a book, or applying for a new job, or creating a new business, if you want to have a much better chance of returning a positive outcome, then you need to know who you're selling to and what they think.

Oh, and just because you think you know your audience doesn't mean that's true.

Febreze, the air freshener, was a huge flop until they did the data research. Proctor & Gamble (P&G) KNEW they had a winner when their research team had accidentally found a chemical that would pull odor away from the source.

They began testing it and came to the conclusion that people would buy it if they marketed it as an odor-remover. Sounds perfectly logical, right?

Well, after a few months of testing it was not selling.

This failure led them to understand that they were marketing the product incorrectly. Specifically, that people loved the product, but using it in the way they were marketing it required a person to change their habits, which is very, very hard to do.

The breakthrough came when Febreze finally understood if they asked potential customers to simply add it to their existing routine, they would adopt it.

And boy did it work. Sales doubled within two months and reached $230 million a year later. And today it has made P&G billions.

Essentially, what P&G did wrong the first time was them saying to their customer, "Your house smells." A customer then thinks, "Buying Febreze means I'm a dirty person."

Nobody wants to admit that, even if it is true. But they didn't realize that until they talked to the customer!

The solution was to market it as an enhancement to your already established routine, not as an odor killer. When you finish vacuuming or doing the laundry, use Febreze to "complete the task".

Back to you and your business, your life, or your career. How can you apply this lesson?

Trying to get promoted at work by "fixing" a broken process? Guess what? Your boss doesn't think it's broken, so trying to force them into changing their habit isn't going to endear you to them come raise time.

Why not instead try to enhance the already established routine? Instead of having a meeting with them saying, "Your process is wrong." Have a meeting that says, "Here's what we currently do. Here's how we can make it better."

Enhance the existing habit. Don't try to destroy it.

I made this mistake a lot when I was elected. In fact, it's one of the biggest reasons why I lost my reelection attempt.

The day I took office I started running full speed to change the system because in my view it was really broken. And it was, truly. But what I didn't realize is that the residents, the voters, didn't really agree. Sure, they said they wanted change, but when it came down to actually pushing change through, they rejected it.

What I should have done is not try to change people's habits so much, and instead start to enhance them, at a slower pace. I paid for it, but I won't make that mistake again.

* * *

Unskippable Brands Aren't Totally Under The Influence

Ahh, influencers. We have this vision in our heads of who they are and it's so glamorous. You wake up every morning, grab your phone, and people pay you to talk about their products and services on your social media channels. Who doesn't want a gig like that?

It's so glamorous that, according to a study by Awin, being a social media influencer is the second most popular career aspiration among those between the ages of 11 and 16 (second only to doctor).

As a brand we love the concept of working with influencers because it's quick and easy, just like buying an ad. Step 1. find an influencer that has an audience that can relate to what you do. Step 2. engage (pay) the influencer and pay them to talk about your product/service. Step 3. collect your millions!

What brands do, incorrectly, is look for influencers with the most followers. But is that really the best way to approach it?

According to an article on BusinessInsider.com, influencers are divided into the following categories.

- Mega: 1 million-plus
- Macro: 200,000 to 900,000 followers
- Midi: 50,000 to 200,000 followers
- Micro: 10,000 to 50,000 followers
- Nano: 800 to 10,000 followers

To most people it just makes sense that if you want to get the most bang for your buck you would reach out to work with the mega influencers who can reach more people.

But when you really think about it, the decision to work

with influencers on the micro and nano level actually makes a lot more sense. And here's why.

When Kim Kardashian (a mega influencer) posts an update on Instagram about a new skin cream that reduces wrinkles, does her audience really think she uses it herself? Probably not. Therefore, is her influence really effective?

Sure, the company that just dropped $50,000 to pay her assistant to grab her phone and hit "post" probably got a nice direct response bump in sales that morning, and maybe even made back that $50,000, and more, but how did that mention really affect long-term sales or help endear the brand to the customer and create loyalty?

Don't kid yourself. It didn't.

Is the influencer bubble bursting? Maybe, maybe not. You make the call. In June of 2019 an influencer named @Arii with 2 million followers failed to sell the 36 T-shirts required for her to start a clothing line.

Let's do the quick math. She has 2 million followers. Let's be really fair and say that only 10 percent of her followers saw the post asking to buy a T-shirt. So that's still 200,000 eyeballs. Now let's say she ended up selling only 30 T-shirts (she needed to sell 36).

30 sales from 200,000 "views" is a conversion rate of 0.00015 percent. Maybe you're not a marketing pro so let me spell it out for you. That is horrendous. Not even one percent! Not even close to one percent.

So what does this mean? Could it mean the t-shirts were just not good? Yes. Could it mean that her audience of followers are broke? Yes. But could it also just mean that maybe she doesn't have as much "influence" as she thought she did? Probably.

Maybe she just wanted to get attention by making the entire thing up? If so, well played @Arii. You got in this book, send me a T-shirt. 2xl please.

Look, buying "influence" from influencers is paid media. It's advertising. Period. You exchange money for exposure. Let's stop talking about it as if it's anything other than that, ads. Ads are fine. Ads work. You should try ads if you haven't already. Done right they can move your needle in the right direction.

But the long game that you should be shooting for, the opportunity to purposely attract a lifetime, loyal customer, isn't going to come from a Tweet from a reality TV show personality. It's going to come from your brand story, told more authentically through an influencer who is trusted, not just known.

We've reached the point in time when a consumer can sniff out an advertisement from 100 miles away. That's especially true for Millennials and Generation Z, who not only can spot the ad, but also reject it as just that, an ad.

In other words, skip it! This lack of trust is why there's a shift of going back to the grassroots level of influence, or as some call "peer-to-peer referrals."

Working with smaller, or macro/micro influencers is really what you want to focus on if buying influence is your game. Now, how to find them? Here are a few ideas.

Look for brand fans. A brand fan is someone who is already advocating for your brand, even at the tiniest level. Pull up your social media and see who is following you; who already loves you. It would be very difficult to reach out to people who don't know who you are, right? So approach these brand fans, who already like and trust you, with an opportunity to advocate for you.

Look for followers that have at least 1,000 followers, and up to 100,000 followers. Maybe you'll find an executive in your space that has a popular podcast and/or blog? Maybe you'll find a foodie who posts images of food on Instagram that has legions of followers looking for the next big foodie trend?

Maybe you'll find nothing, but at least you looked.

Hopefully you find some good candidates, now what? Don't just contact them and offer them money. Start a conversation with them.

Let's use the foodie example. You are a new restaurant in the area and you need to get some attention. Find the local foodie influencer and invite them in for a special dinner from your chef.

Be very clear you're hoping that they will talk about their experience. You could offer them, in addition, future free meals or discounts for them or to give away to their followers.

This all seems like a ton of work, right? But this is how it's done. Remember we talked about getting out of the Yellow Pages Mentality? This is a perfect example.

Should you just "buy an ad" from an influencer; that's not going to work in most cases. I would also strongly suggest you look at who the influencer has promoted before and try to determine if it actually worked or not.

Here's a tip, check out Fanjoy.co or Izea.com for good resources to find influencers.

Another way to find brand fans is to simply go to Google and type in a hashtag. Example: #clevelandfood. Chances are you probably already know what the popular hashtags are for your area and business. Search those hashtags daily for brand fans that are passionate and begin communicating with them. But always first find out how many followers they have and what kind of posts they usually publish.

Unskippable Content Is Authentic & Candid, Not Planned & Perfected

As with all of my books, I try really hard to not write about specific social media platforms only because history has proven that as the years go by, platforms change dramatically. What we talk about today might not even be around tomorrow, or a few years from now.

That being said, let's just talk about authenticity, and we'll use Instagram as an example, at this current point in time (2019).

Instagram now has 1 billion monthly active users, and 500 million daily active users. Not too shabby. But like most social media platforms, especially one so flagrantly used by influencers, what works on Instagram changes faster than you can keep up with.

For example, when Instagram really took off in 2017 - 2018, it became a platform for perfectly framed and lit photos. Influencers would spend hours on photo shoots trying to take that perfect shot of their dog on the beach at sunset in the hopes of millions of likes and new followers, and it worked.

But it's 2019, and times have changed. Influencer overload is upon us, and authenticity is what people care about.

This reminds me of a time before YouTube. Back then, if you produced a low-quality video you were considered unprofessional. So, you spent $40,000 on a professionally made video to show how important you were.

But then Youtube came along and after a few years, and some help from the fact that almost every person had a phone with a video camera in it, a video that is over produced is not wanted. It's fake. It's skippable.

What we're seeing when you look at the history of The Internet as a whole is when things initially launch they are usually adopted first in the ways we previously viewed how business works.

But what happens is that after some time, what matters most is authenticity and the shift occurs.

Back to Instagram. In an article on TheAtlantic.com called *The Instagram Aesthetic Is Over*, they quote a Los Angeles–based influencer named Sarah Peretz, who fell victim to the aesthetic trap. "I spent so many months looking for a wall that was a certain color (for my photos)," Peretz said. "There came a point in my life where all I'd be looking for was walls, walls, walls. I was like, *Guess what day it is? It's another wall.*"

All for a perfect photo for likes. We can debate the validity of that business plan in another book (probably not). The point is that finding the perfect wall for a post is no longer effective.

$$* * *$$

Authenticity Always Makes You Unskippable

Nowadays, influencers are rising in the ranks by providing messier, unfiltered photos and videos. I had to prove this theory for myself so I grabbed my 17 year-old daughter's phone (which I pay for, so I can do whatever I want with it) and I start looking through her feed.

What I found was proof of authenticity. In fact, a LOT of what is posted now is photos and video that are really poor quality. I mean, less than average. It's almost as if they're going out of their way to make their photos look worse.

Actually, that's exactly what they're doing.

There's an app called Huji Cam that helps take photos as if it were "just like the year 1998." What it does is take a photo that looks like it came from a pre-Internet real, crap camera.

Does anyone, besides me, see the irony in the fact that people crave authenticity, yet they are cool with an app that distorts a photo to make it look like something it's not? But I digress.

We're almost to the finish line on this topic, bear with me.

Here's the good news. The really good news. Through all

of this influencer stuff, and all of the wishy-washy trends of what's cool and what's not cool, comes the truth.

And the truth is that people are willing to follow someone who isn't faking it, and who is willing to post real, authentic content that shows who they are in even their most unflattering form.

Authenticity ALWAYS wins, in the long run. And that is awesome.

Now back to you. We both know that you've probably tried to present yourself or your business in an inauthentic way at some point. You didn't do it to fool people. You did it because you thought that in order to reach them you had to talk to them a certain way.

I'll admit it, I've done it, only because I thought that that was the way to best communicate with my buyers, which of course, was completely wrong.

Only after years and years of learning what my audience wanted, and finally giving myself permission to be myself, was I able to truly make a connection with them.

The most Unskippable companies you run into all live through an authentic mindset. Through their marketing and their products and services. Through their customer service.

It's the ones that aren't true that we choose to forget or not do business with.

Unskippable Brands Survive By Being More Awesome Than The Other Awesome Competitors

You would think that a company like Costco would be feeling the pinch from Amazon like all the others, but they're not. In fact they are growing by leaps and bounds financially.

Besides the financial growth, I was also surprised to find out that 81 percent of Costco employees would recommend working at Costco to a friend. As it turns out, the culture they have cultivated inside the walls there makes for a pretty amazing business.

But that's not the only reason.

To be successful in business you have to worry about two groups. First, your consumers. Second, your employees. And Costco worries, a lot, about them both. In the latest American Customer Satisfaction Index, or ACSI, Costco became the #1 business for overall customer satisfaction.

Guess who they beat? You were right, Amazon!

So, Costco is nailing it on both ends. Why? Let's start with their customers. And while you're reading this, please think about your business. Do you do these things? Are you customer and employee obsessed?

From the Costco website, here is their ideology.

Commitment to quality. Costco warehouses carry about 4,000 SKUs (stock keeping units) compared to the 30,000 found at most supermarkets. By carefully choosing products based on quality, price, brand, and features, the company can offer the best value to members.

QUALITY: I am a Costco member, and one of the things I love about shopping there is I know that whatever I buy is going to be amazing. Not just good, but amazing.

I can't tell you how many times I've bought a bag of chips, or turkey burgers or a pair of socks and I've been extremely happy with it, to the point where I say out loud to my wife, "Those chips/burgers from Costco were amazing. Next time we go back we have to buy those again."

Hopefully everything you sell, whether it's a product or a service, is amazing, right?

NO RISK: Another reason is there's no risk involved. On the very few occasions where I've not been blown away by the product, I simply return it with their no-questions asked policy.

I have a friend who bought a tree at Costco, and it died a year later. He put it in the back of his truck and took it back and returned it. A dead tree! They didn't blink an eye or argue. Just gave him another tree.

When there is no pain/risk of purchase you eliminate objections to a sale. Amazon is great. But, if you get something you don't like, you still have to follow their return policies, which is usually to print out the label for shipping, then find a box to pack it in, put the label on, go to the post office, etc.

Remember the last time someone bought something from you and you argued with them because they wanted a return? How'd that work out for you? You spent time and energy debating with them about it, and in the end, you probably got blasted on social media.

Over what? You were right and they were wrong? It's against our return policy!!! Just give them their money back and move on and be better for it.

SELECTION: I have no issues that Costco doesn't carry 30,000 SKUs like a normal grocery store, in fact, I find that lack of choice simpler. It means I don't have to make a million decisions when I shop there.

Think about going to your local grocery store to buy peanut butter. In my local store there are literally 15 different options to buy.

At Costco, there's usually just one. Buy it, or don't. People don't like to have to make too many decisions.

You don't have to sell everything. In fact, it's better when you don't. Ever walk into a coffee shop and see scores of shelves for coffee related products like actual coffee makers? Nobody is buying a coffee maker in a coffee shop. I came here because I don't want to make coffee at home!

Note: The third largest grocery chain in the USA, Aldi, does the exact same thing. From an article on CNN, when they asked an Aldi shopper why they like shopping there they said, "I'm a busy mom. I don't have time to navigate a huge grocery store with kids begging to get out and go home. I can get in and out of an Aldi in no time. I'm not sifting through 50 different varieties of salsa."

Entrepreneurial spirit. Throughout the decades, the entrepreneurial drive for excellence has continued to define Costco staff at every level. From its management team to the people on the warehouse floor, everyone is united in a common goal to exceed member expectations.

I feel that sense of community and pride when I shop at

Costco. Not so much when I'm at my local grocery store where a 16 year-old kid is working the checkout line and I can tell by the look on his face he'd rather be anywhere else in the world.

Costco people are friendly, and just seem to care more. It's like they're all a team and I can feel that when I shop there.

Employee focus. Costco is often noted for being much more employee-focused than other Fortune 500 companies. By offering fair wages and top-notch benefits, the company has created a workplace culture that attracts positive, high-energy, talented employees.

You've got to keep your employees happy if you want to become Unskippable. You know this, so I won't belabor the point.

The question is, are you actually doing something about it and giving them what they want?

Summary: Be like Costco. Be Unskippable.

I will tell you this last thing about Aldi and Costco. I shop at both places often for my lunch and I get there right before they open in the morning. Every single time I go to either place there is a giant line of people waiting to get in. I never see that at the big grocery store across the street.

* * *

Unskippable People Create Alter Egos To Push Themselves To New Limits

If you haven't picked up a copy of Todd Herman's book *The Alter Ego Effect* yet, then you should grab one.

Essentially, Herman argues that if you want to excel or perform at peak levels, then you need to create what is called an alter ego, a second self, that gives you the power to accomplish your goals.

That's my description. Here's his.

"In *The Alter Ego Effect*, Herman shows you how to activate the Heroic Self already nested inside of each of us, through countless stories from salespeople, executives, entertainers, athletes, entrepreneurs, creatives and historical figures. He reveals that you may not be using those traits in the moments when you need them the most."

Let's unpack this concept a bit.

First off, creating an alter ego isn't about being fake or untrue to yourself. Your authenticity, in the performance world, is linked to your stage persona. Beyonce isn't the same person she is at home when she's on stage performing for thousands of fans or when she's a guest on The Tonight Show.

It's not fake or unauthentic for an introvert to mentally trick their brain into being an extrovert when the stage lights come on. You're still you. You're just a different you, for a short time.

Here's how I have been using his advice. When I'm alone in my office working, or at home, I'm a completely different person than I am when I'm in front of a client or on the stage speaking.

Why? Because I know I have to be "on" when I'm working or presenting in front of an audience. Even before I had read Herman's book, I was semi-consciously creating an alter ego in those situations so that I would "perform" at a higher level.

But what I was not really doing was giving that alter ego a name and a mission. So using Herman's advice I created a completely new persona called "Johnny Showtime".

I know, what a completely ridiculous name. But to me, it's the person that is ready to be "on" and ready to perform.

The moment I get out of my car to walk into a client's office, or the second I walk out of my hotel room in Vegas to hit the stage, I become Johnny Showtime, in my head.

Johnny is me of course, but Johnny's main goal is to deliver a performance, where regular Jim Kukral is a laid back and not typically a performer.

What exactly do I do different? This could mean things as small as aggressive and friendly networking with attendees of the event pre and post speaking. That could mean being extra personable to the event coordinators, and going out of my way to be helpful and appreciative.

And of course, being a dynamic and engaging performer on stage in front of an audience, or in a conference room.

I've never been much of an athlete, but I get the concept (as most do) of game day mode. For game day mode, I take all of my other thoughts about the other parts of my life and I put them in a chamber and lock them up, and focus only on the task at hand, which is winning the game, at that moment.

Then, as soon as I'm back in my hotel room or back in my office (the game is over), I'm back to my normal self.

I should have been a psychiatrist because I find how the human brain works to be fascinating. One of the things I found out when researching this book and reading Herman's book was a thing called "Enclothed cognition."

Researchers at Northwestern University have found that the clothing we wear affects our psychological states, as well as our performance levels. Given their findings, individuals can intentionally choose to wear clothing that will induce more desirable psychological states and enhance task-related performance.

Or to simplify it: You put on a cape and you become a superhero.

Why does this work? Because humans think with their brains, and bodies.

In an article on PositivePsycologyNews.com, "Cognitive psychologists Hajo Adam and Adam Galinksy from North-western University have been examining the psychological and performance-related effects that wearing specific arti-cles of clothing have on the person wearing them.

Enclothed cognition captures the systematic influence that clothes have on the wearer's psychological processes. It is part of a larger field of research that examines how humans think with both their brains and their bodies, an area of study known as *embodied cognition*.

Embodied cognition experts have discovered that our thought processes are based on physical experiences that set off associated abstract concepts, including those generated by the clothing we wear. Clothing can enhance our psycho-logical states, and it can improve our performance on tasks."

My friend Joe Pulizzi does this with the color orange. He wears orange shoes, and orange shirts, and orange ties. He even has a complete orange suit that he'll wear on stage! On top of that, he has a wonderful charitable organization called "The Orange Effect" that helps children with speech disorders get the therapy and technology they need.

My other friend, Facebook Marketing Guru, Mari Smith, does this with turquoise.

Professional speaker and best-selling author Jay Baer wears plaid suits when he performs on stage. He even let's his audience choose which plaid suit they want him to wear! Check that out at www.dressjaybaer.com.

I love the color blue so I have chosen to incorporate that into my alter ego. I own a pair of blue rimmed glasses that I wear, and I have blue shirts and blue shoes that I wear when I perform.

Beside the benefit of building a brand with this technique, you also get your audience involved. Pulizzi's love of orange at his conferences started to catch on and all of a sudden people were showing up wearing all kinds of orange clothing with everyone trying to outdo the other.

This created a tribe of people who shared in on the fun. And when you create a tribe organically like this, good things happen.

How can you do it? Here's a checklist of things you can do to help you get started with creating an Alter Ego.

#1 - Create a persona, and name him/her

#2 - Choose a color, or article of clothing that defines that persona (fun hat, glasses, etc.)

#3 - Decide when that persona's goals are when they are activated

Okay, now you've got a basic starting point; there's way more to it. Go put it into effect the next time you're trying to make a sale, or applying for a job, or whatever it is you're doing.

It might just be the thing that helps you get over the mental hurdle and on the path to a positive outcome.

* * *

Unskippable Businesses Focus On One Thing, & One Thing Only?

 "The way to become rich is to put all your eggs in one basket and then watch that basket." - Andrew Carnegie.

What's in your basket?

Are you a real estate agent in Maine, but you also do the books for a taxidermist? There's nothing wrong with having two jobs of course.

But if you really think about it, how can you be the absolute best at one thing, if you're doing both things?

Here's my pushback on the Andrew Carnegie quote above.

Is life really about being the best at everything? Do you

really have to force yourself to focus on one goal in life? That sounds horrible.

Here's what you must do.

You MUST do what you love and have a passion for.

You MUST do whatever you need to do to pay your bills and feed your family.

You MUST live your life how you want and quit listening to business gurus telling you that making a ton of money is what will make you happy.

How many business books have you read that told you in order to be successful you must focus on one thing and one thing only.

Here's a story. I've got a friend with a mind that can focus like none other. From the time she was out of college she started multiple businesses with laser focus in each of them. She made a lot of money from that focus.

Her problem? She hated what she was doing. So she got very wealthy doing what she hated and then, years later, realized the money was nice, but meant nothing. She hadn't built something she cared about.

Ultimately, that's what she figured out after time - that life is too short to do things you don't give a crap about.

Today she runs a business that helps people adopt cats. She created a cafe where people can have some coffee and relax, but hang out with cats, with the ultimate goal of hopefully adopting them. Every day she goes to work knowing that she could potentially match up a person with a cat in a forever home.

The money isn't that great - nowhere near what she used to do, but she's okay with it. The laser focus she used to put on her businesses that she didn't care about is now on the new business, and it's successful because of it.

The difference is now she can wake up every day happy to do what she does.

Ask yourself this important question. What is more important to you, the money, or doing what you love to do?

Sure, it's possible to have both, but when it comes down to the choice and you can't have both, which one do you choose?

You're going to be Unskippable to yourself based upon the decisions you make. Choose wisely.

Unskippable People Define Their Own Success

From birth we're taught that we need to do the following. Go to school then get a job that we probably don't like because we have to work to make money to buy all the things that we must have in order to be happy.

Sigh.

Most of us believe that stuff, but some of us do not.

Right now you're reading this and maybe you have followed that script, and maybe you're working at a job that you don't have passion for. You feel stuck because you have bills to pay and a family to support.

Maybe you have tons of college loan debt, or you bought too big of a house and it's slowly eating your savings?

How can you change things? How do you fix your life through your career?

The easy answer is to tell you to quit and start your own business doing something that you are passionate about. But many of you don't want to be entrepreneurs, and I get that.

Then what?

Let's start at the benefit as good salespeople always do. We choose to eat kale because the benefit is health, not taste. Yuck. We buy Apple products because they "just work" but also as the benefit of "status".

The point is we choose to do things because of the direct or indirect benefits we get from them.

That being said. You work, in a job you hate, because you need money, so you can be happy.

Happy, happy, happy.

Money, money, money.

Money = happiness, right?

Are you happy, really? When you wake up in the morning are you springing out of bed to rush to your job? Chances are you are not.

What I want you to do right now is come up with a list of jobs you wish you had that would make you feel that excitement and joy every morning. Stop reading, and write them down.

Is what you're currently doing on that list? No? That's a problem.

* * *

What Happened To Us?

If you go back hundreds of years ago you will find that most people didn't work as much as we do now. In medieval times peasants worked at a leisurely pace with afternoon nap breaks and slow lunches.

They weren't rich in wealth by any means, but they were rich in leisure.

Did you know that the United States is the only advanced country without a national vacation policy? That sums it up pretty well.

A study by the Center for American Progress noted that "Americans consider a 40 hour work week as part time in most professional jobs and as a sign of a stagnant career."

That's messed up. In fact, as the report concludes, the monetary reward for working longer hours has increased significantly over the past 30 years.

Or another way of putting that conclusion: If you work your ass off you'll make more money and won't be a "loser."

Stop for a second and really consider that thought. You're a loser if you don't make a lot of money and you don't work so much you cause a heart attack and neglect your family and friends?

There is nothing wrong with hard work. Some people are workaholics and they enjoy the grind and the day-to-day hustle. Their religion is the hustle and their heaven is a fat bank account.

Like I said earlier, that's fine if that's what you want. But for most people, it's not.

Younger people don't buy into the money equals happiness mantra. CNBC reports that the majority of young people have less than $1,000 in their savings accounts, and a significant number have nothing at all.

They spend their money on "comforts and conveniences" like ride sharing, fancy coffee and eating lunch and dinner.

I've argued before that people who have grown up in a post 9/11 world have different attitudes. That the world could end tomorrow so why fret? Or they've seen their parents struggle for money and realize they don't want to be in that position in this very difficult economy.

Regardless of the reason, the fact remains that they don't see a lack of financial wealth as being a loser; they see it as a badge of honor of sorts.

Unskippable People Have A Life Purpose & Live Longer Because Of It

A new study published on the Jama Network Open asked the question, "Does an association exist between life purpose and mortality among people older than 50 years?"

The results from studying almost 7,000 adults says yes, there is a correlation.

More specifically, the report states that people without a strong life purpose, which was defined as "a self-organizing life aim that stimulates goals," were more likely to die sooner than people who had a life purpose.

Translation: Care about something important to you and you're passionate about and pursue it, because you'll live longer.

The study didn't ask what their life purpose was, only if they had one.

Maybe for you it's raising children, like it is for me. Maybe for you it's running a successful business and making a ton of money, that's fine. Maybe for you it's simply having a nice, calm life without pressure or material possessions? Even better.

Whatever it is for you, it's time to go do it before the clock stops ticking. Tick, tick, tick..

Unskippable Winners vs. Losers

Here's a list of some things that society has told us that makes us winners in life.

We're winners if we can afford to eat out at a fancy Italian restaurant.

But you know what? The experience of eating Italian food in Italy sounds like a better life goal doesn't it? If only you stopped spending so much of your income on restaurants and saved it for a plane ticket?

We're winners if we drive a Mercedes or other expensive ride.

But you know what? The experience of not having a car payment is better.

We're winners if we went to an Ivy League school.

But you know what? The experience of not having a few hundred thousand dollars on student loans to pay off is probably a happier one.

We're winners if we have a high-paying job.

But you know what? The experience of making less money, and doing something you love is what you'll remember on your deathbed looking back on your life.

Are you happy right now? Do your possessions enhance your life, or make it more difficult? Hate your job? Do you feel like a loser when you can't afford to live in that mcmansion around the corner?

We are only on this Earth for a blip. It might be time to start rejecting what society has taught you and start going on your own path to happiness.

Unskippable People Count Their Blessings, Not Their Burdens

To further this point, a study done by the Department of Psychology, University of California, found people that are consciously grateful for the blessings in their lives are happier than the people who focus on the hassles in their lives.

In other words, if you're always focusing on the hassles and burdens, you're only going to find your life a hassle/burden.

Duh, right? Unfortunately this logical conclusion is something that many of us are unable to practice for our own reasons.

I would ask you now though, after being presented with this information, are you going to change the way you view your life, or not? Are you going to continue to focus on the hassles and the burdens?

Or are you going to change your mind right now, this very second, and start focusing on the blessings in your life? Your choice. Choose wisely. Your happiness depends on it.

* * *

Unskippable People See The Positive; Skippable People Are Blind To It

We've all got that one friend. You know, they're the Debbie Downer in your life. Everything that happens to them is the fault of someone else. They are constantly negative and only see the bad things around them.

This is because they choose to only see the negative. Because of this they live their life full of stress, regret and bitterness, instead of peace, fulfillment and joy.

Which person do you want to be? Hopefully you're not Debbie Downer, but maybe you are trying to be better, like most of us.

Paulo Coelho, international best-selling author said, "The world is changed by your example, not by your opinion."

Here's how you start changing things for yourself. Here's how to lead by example for a better world for yourself and those around you.

Start looking for yellow cars.

The Yellow Car Phenomenon isn't anything new, but you probably haven't heard of it. It's based on neuroscience. Essentially, it boils down to this.

Once you start opening your mind to the idea of seeing yellow cars, you'll see them more.

Some people also call this the Baader–Meinhof effect, or frequency illusion. It's the illusion in which a word, a name, or other thing that has recently come to one's attention suddenly seems to appear with improbable frequency shortly afterwards.

Here's another example. Once you start opening your eyes to seeing billboards, you'll see them more. Replace yellow cars and billboards with anything in your life. It's logical, really. If you are mentally cognizant of something, you will see it more.

Open your mind, Neo. The Matrix is real, and it's a wonderful place "if" you're looking for the right things.

Once you start opening your mind to seeing businesses having success in your industry, you can begin to see your clear path to that same, or better, success.

Once you start opening your mind to seeing positive people in your life, you can begin to see a clear path to achieving that same positivity.

Once you start opening your mind to focusing on opportunities and friendships, you will begin to see more doors open to you and more friends appearing.

It's all about what you CHOOSE to focus on.

On the flip side, if you keep looking for the negative, then that's all you're going to see. If you keep watching cable news and only see the fighting, disruption and divisiveness, that's all you're going to absorb, and manifest through your own business, life or career.

If you continue to blame everyone else for the problems in your life, then you're never going to understand it's the people who rise above that mentality, take responsibility for their own issues, and who are the ones that are happy, healthy and full of joy.

This is all based on RAS, or as the super-smart people call it, The Reticular Activating System. The RAS is a collection of nerves in your brainstem that filter out unnecessary information (the skippable stuff) so the essential stuff (the Unskippable stuff) makes it through.

Imagine you're at a crowded, loud event and your spouse is

trying to get your attention from across the room, so they yell out your name. The RAS is the reason you can filter out and hear that call. First, you're hearing it in a familiar voice/tone that you have already accepted into your brain. Second, it's your name, so you're already conditioned to responding to it.

The RAS is your filter to the world you want to live in. And it's not just auditory or sight based. It's your filter for your feelings and your beliefs. I'm a believer that people cannot change their lives or their behaviors until they really want to change.

If you're a smoker and you really don't want to stop smoking, you're not going to quit successfully. You may say you want to quit, but mentally, you're just not ready to do it. You have to be ready to want to change, and then, and only then will your RAS let you filter the messages into your brain so you can make it happen.

And usually, it's an experience, good or bad, that causes that mindset change. An example would be having a health issue caused by smoking.

Understanding this will not only help you achieve your best self, but also aid in how to deal with your co-workers, or employees, or boss, or customers or friends/family.

Remember, you cannot force someone to change until they are ready and open to it. Trying otherwise will cause you a lot of stress, pain and time. Instead, focus on the people and customers in your life that see the world in the same way that you do.

Only then will you become Unskippable in your business, life or career.

* * *

Are You Feeling Unskippable Yet?

66 *"However ordinary each of us may seem, we are all in some way special, and can do things that are extraordinary, perhaps until then...even thought impossible."* - Sir Roger Bannister

Ready to run your record-breaking, four-minute mile?

Here's an interesting follow up to the story of the Unskippable Roger Bannister.

Do you know why they call him "Sir" Roger Bannister? It's because he was knighted for his world-record accomplishment in 1975 (29 years later) by the Queen of England.

But Sir Roger's story didn't end after he broke the record; far from it. After he completed his medical studies, he spent the next two decades as a neurologist and clinical researcher affecting the lives of thousands of people through medicine.

In addition, his autobiography *First Four Minutes*, was published in 1955 and inspired millions of people around the globe.

He then went on to become Master of Pembroke College at Oxford, before retiring in 1993. Sir Roger passed away peacefully at his home, surrounded by his family in 2018.

That's a pretty Unskippable life don't you think?

This is it, right now. Your journey to becoming Unskippable has already begun. It's time to make your choice. The choice between creating a positive mindset shift and changing your business, your life, or your career.

Or, simply ignoring everything you just read and going back to your current way of thinking, and doing (or not doing). Deep down in your heart you know what you need to do.

The only thing stopping you from making it happen is your belief that what you really want in this life is impossible.

It's not.

Four years ago I thought it would be impossible that I could run for public office and win an election and serve my community.

Ten years ago I thought it would be impossible for me to have written 10 books, or to have a career inspiring people from the stage.

Twenty years ago I thought it would be impossible to be an entrepreneur and run my own successful business and have an amazing family.

Thirty years ago I thought it would be impossible for me to graduate high school, let alone earn a college degree.

But all of those things happened.

You begin the journey to becoming Unskippable in your business, life or career when you start believing that the impossible, is possible.

Thank you for reading #Unskippable

* * *

W ill you help me get to 500 reviews?

If you loved this book, or even just liked it a little, now is the time where I would ask you to please go and leave a review wherever you bought it, or if you got a free copy, do the same!

Reviews are the lifeblood of books like this and I would consider it a personal favor. I am on a quest to get 500 reviews of this book and I can only do it with your help.

I would also ask you to share the book to your followers on social media or your blog or email list. Make sure to use the hashtag #Unskippable.

If you would like me to appear on your podcast or radio show or webinar to talk about the book, I'd be happy to do that as well.

Feel free to reach out to me with a text at (216) 236-8294. I respond to every single one! Hope to hear from you!

* * *

Want To Write An Unskippable Book With Me?

I'm looking for serious, dedicated subject-matter experts in ALL industries to potentially write a new book in partnership with me under the Unskippable brand.

Example: You are a top real estate agent or dentist or social media expert in your field (pick any vertical you're a professional in). You have a proven track record of success and you have a story to tell and the desire to have a book about it.

In other words, you are, and you understand, what makes people and businesses Unskippable in your industry.

Is this you? Go to www.JimKukral.com/writewithjim and let's have a conversation.

ADDENDUM (DON'T SKIP THIS)

The following are the full transcripts of the interviews I did with some really smart people who helped me with this book.

You have already read some of their thoughts sprinkled throughout the book in the appropriate places, but I thought it would be helpful to include the full conversations below.

There are tons of gold nuggets here. Don't skip this.

Unskippable People Manifest Success Through Positivity

Here's an interview I did with the Morning Coach, JB Glossinger. A Ph.D in Metaphysics, JB has been motivating people for over 15-years through his daily CoachCast podcast with over 3,500 episodes and 26 million downloads.

He has helped countless people get organized, focused, and become their best self. He's pretty Unskippable. Checkout Morningcoach.com if you need some motivation in your life.

Jim: I say there are two types of people in the world, skippable people and Unskippable people and you've coached a lot of people. You've talked to a lot of people. What do people really want? Is it money? Happiness?

JB Glossinger: Yeah, I think initially people want money, which is funny. When I first started coaching I had no money, right? So I talk to a lot of people that didn't have money and that they thought money would bring them happiness.

Now in my career I attract a much more successful person who tends to have multi-layer problems, which typically are children or family issues - things that money can't solve. So, there are a couple different types of people out there. The people that are broke are trying to figure it out, like I was. I get it. And money really does solve their problems.

So, anybody that says money doesn't solve his or her problems, it would. Get them a new house, get them their car, get them some freedom. And then there's another set of people that are dealing with some significant issues that are successful already but are dealing with societal pressures, fame issues, performance issues and that's where I've kind of tended to go to now is dealing with all those people.

Jim: Why do so many people equate money to happiness? I mean, I get it, you need money to live your life and be able to do things, but at what point does that become a toxic mindset?

JB: Well, I think it's a sign of pressure. I just think it's keeping up with the Joneses'. It's what we're conditioned with every day. If you're not successful, if you don't accumulate things.

You know I've been very blessed to have Wayne Dyer in my life before he passed away and writing for Hay House and meeting some people that are a little bit more enlightened and the fact that that isn't what they care about.

I mean I don't want to sit here and say money is not important, because like I said, for a lot of people that don't have money it does solve their issues. But money being everything that somebody's after is what really causes problems.

Everybody has problems. Everybody. And whatever that solution is going to be a little extra money or finding some happiness or getting mental help, I haven't met anybody who doesn't have something going on in your life that's an issue. Just everybody does.

Jim: Have you noticed like I have, that around 2015 became kind of the tipping point of social media and toxicity and I think it just has gotten to a point where people have just become so exhausted with all the negativity. That's why I think your stuff is gonna explode and continue it explode because people want more of a positive view on things.

JB: I would agree. I think people are tired of the social media political stuff. It's just so in depth and negative now, I think that you just have people that are tired of it. Society is just really negative.

Jim: Let's talk a little bit about mindset. Can you really affect change in your life and your business, your life, your career, without changing your mindset?

JB: I think it's all in your head. I mean it really is. I mean perception is reality and you know if you go throughout your day and think that the business world is bad and you're not gonna make any money and things aren't gonna work. You're gonna get that.

But if you can say, look, there are a lot of negative people out there, but I can optimistically change my life. There are billions of people in the world and I'll find the right ones who want to work with me. That mindset is gonna serve you better.

Now are there times to be analytical and be negative, yes, I believe that when you make major decisions in your life that you need to look at the worst possible outcome and realize you can handle that.

You don't want to manifest it, but I think you have to be a rational human being. You can't be some myopic person just thinking everything around you is gonna be positive, but I think that that mindset shift will serve you so much more than a negative one.

Jim: Why is it so hard for people to change mindset? If you're a negative person are you always gonna be negative person or can you change that?

JB: I think there's a couple things going on. One is chemical. For men, for example, or women, estrogen and hormonal differences are huge. So, anybody over 40, if their testosterone drops to 200, alternately they're gonna be negative.

They're like an 80 year-old man. It's really hard. There are some chemical issues going on there and I think then the other side of it is being able to get around the right people and get out of the negative conditioning because if you're in the news cycle, it's almost impossible.

I'm not the most positive person you'll meet but if I sit down and watch CNN hour after hour, I'm gonna be negative. I think the world is going to end. And so it's really challenging in the society we live in, especially with Facebook and Snapchat and Twitter.

We have people right now complaining about Game of Thrones that they need to rewrite it. There's people literally protesting a TV show.

Jim: A TV show based on complete fiction.

JB: Correct. Millions of people are spending their emotional energy signing petitions to redo the show. To me that is a sickness. It's almost a disease.

It's like where is your brain at? Are you really a happy, balanced, fulfilled person if you're worried about Game of Thrones and having them rewrite it?

Jim: Let me read you this quote and then we'll react to it. "You will continue to suffer if you have an emotional reaction to everything that is said to you. True power is sitting back in observing things with logic."

JB: I agree 100 percent. It's all about observation. We're here for a very small amount of time - less than a hundred years if we're lucky to go that far. So, you've got to observe and understand life.

I'm turning 50 in a couple of weeks and it's really a transitional period for me because that's some significant age. And I see things a lot differently than I used to and a lot of it has to do with the emotion and understanding emotion.

Stepping back and realizing why am I feeling the way I'm feeling, why am I letting this bother me? Why am I worried that Daenerys (Mother of Dragons) was killed on Game of Thrones? Do I really care that much about that or in three months is that gonna be gone forever in my life?

Understanding those emotions and being able to observe what you're doing and why you're doing it is paramount to having a really good life.

Jim: Yeah, I totally agree with you. A couple of more things. I was reading this report by OnePoll and they said the average American hasn't made a new friend in five years according to this study and they mean like a real friend not a Facebook friend.

I think, obviously, that's really sad. And my argument is the emergence of social media has widened our circles so far that we've essentially replaced real friendships with these virtual friendships. That's a problem. Isn't it?

JB: A huge problem. Not only are we not having intimate friends or relationships anymore, but kids that are in their twenties are not even having sex as much. It's the lack of connection anymore, this lack of intimacy that social media has created that people don't even know how to have sex anymore. It's scary.

Jim: Yeah, it's really scary. The last thing I want to talk to you about is a TED talk by Robert Waldinger. He's a psychiatrist from the Harvard School of Adult Development and they did a 75-year study of looking at people's happiness.

They came to one big conclusion and he basically said, 'The clearest message we get from this 75 year study is good relationships keep us happier and healthier." You coach a lot of people. Is this right?

JB: Yes, 100 percent. One of my biggest things and biggest successes over the last couple years has been the masterminds that I put together and getting together with real people. I mean that literally the community is more important than anything else I think I've ever created and I'm learning that more and more.

I'm learning that from a business perspective that I needed to have more boots on the street. It's getting tougher and tougher to convert people from social media or even coaching systems via the Internet. It's more important that I speak and then I talk to real people and I connect with real people. That's what works for me now.

Comparatively, 10 years ago it was so easy to just create a landing page and buy some Facebook ads to convert. All that's changing, all of its changing. And I really think the reason is is because people are getting tired of all that noise and you've got to be able to connect one-on-one. You've got to be able to connect in a real life.

Jim: Yeah. Your current relationships are really important. One of the things I've been dealing with was being elected and I held on to this grudge after I losing my second election.

It's such a personal thing to be elected and then to lose an election from people telling lies about you. That's because it's not like you're marketing some product. It's you.

So, when somebody goes around telling lies about you and then people vote you out of office, which happened to me, it was a very personal thing and I held a grudge for over a year. I found a way to let go of it because that's a bad thing to hold a grudge. Isn't it?

JB: Yeah, it's a poison. Anything that's kind of negative like that is really poison that just eats at you and you have to learn to let go.

In fact, I just was reading Wayne Dyer this morning and I want to read you a quote. I just did it this morning for tomorrow's show and the quote is, "Men are disturbed not by things that happen but by their opinion of things that happen."

Jim: How do you overcome somebody who comes to you who's not ready to make a change? Can that person be convinced?

I guess the question is this, do you have to be mentally ready to make your change to improve your business or your life or your career or can you be forced into it?

JB: I think everybody's different. Every experience is different. Everybody's different. But I do believe, obviously, the more somebody wants to change, the easier it is to happen.

We almost have to have something occur in our lives that, hey, that's it. I'm changing. Now I will tell you from a metaphysical standpoint one of the challenging things is with our family and friends to see them shift is something that they need to check too.

So, the best thing that you can do is if you've got somebody that you're trying to help change who doesn't want to change is to start to see the change in them. And the last resort would be to just let them go. I hate to say that, but sometimes you've got to let people go out of your life.

* * *

Unskippable Brands Create Loyalty Through Positive Experiences

I interviewed professional keynote speaker and best-selling author Andrew Davis for this book. We talked about several different things including loyalty. Here's the transcript of this interview.

Jim Kukral: So I interviewed our friend Mark Schaefer. He's got his new, amazing, *Marketing Rebellion* book out and he said, "Our customers have become our marketing. We're basically in a loyalty-free world." Then he said, "Research shows that 83 percent of customers shop around and only 17 percent are loyal."

Andrew Davis: I can't dispute Mark's data [laughs]. But here's the thing, I think the problem is yes, of course, they shop around. I think the fundamental problem to be honest is that the marketing model we're using is raw.

It's like we're using a funnel concept that it relies on you constantly raising awareness for your brand so that while people are doing research, they come across you, right?

And I think that's a really expensive and slow way to get customers.

I don't think that loyalty is dead by any means. I just think that loyalty needs to be redefined as an experience, not like a membership card or a point system that rewards you with discounts. Like my experiences that brands that deliver a great experience are actually able to convert more customers at higher margins that don't require discounts.

And their customers are unbelievable loyal in the sense that they trust and understand the experience they're going to get from the, you know, the vendor that they've chosen.

So, I don't think we live in a world free of loyalty. I just think we got so hung up on trying to market to new customers in a world where loyalty is changing but we haven't changed the definition of loyalty.

Jim: Well, you know, Payless ShoeSource recently went out of business. They closed all their stores.

Andrew: Yup.

Jim: And I make the argument, it's like what experience did they create for people? It was like, hey, you have to go to the store and buy cheap shoes.

They never sold their own branded products and the experience was just like any other retail experience. So, what you're saying is we have got to go beyond that.

Andrew: Yeah, absolutely. Here's the reason we end up competing on price and features and functions and benefits. It's because we all look and sound the same. The best way to differentiate your product, your service in the market-place is to do something different that makes you stand out. And Payless did nothing different.

You can go online and get cheap shoes without ever leaving the comfort of your house. You can do that in your under-pants and they show up at your door, you try them on, if you don't like them, it's free shipping, you send them back. Payless had to change the experience, especially in the retail world today.

The retailers that are being really successful are building experiences that build loyalty, and that's what's really important.

Jim: Did you watch the show *Mad Men?*

Andrew: Yeah, of course.

Jim: There's a Don Draper quote from the show, one of my favorites, which is, "What you call love was invented by guys like me, to sell nylons."

Andrew: Yes.

Jim: Experiences are emotional, right?

Andrew: Absolutely. Experiences are emotional. In fact, essentially a great experience should have intense and eager, enjoyment, interest, or approval, which is the complete opposite of apathy. And most experiences deliver apathy.

We're so focused on getting the sale and getting the product or the service into the hands or minds of our consumers that we forget that it's after they open the box with the product that we sent them or it's after a walk in the door of that hotel or it's after they get their spa treatment that we've got ensure the experience delivers what we need.

And essentially, the higher the enjoyment and enthusiasm you deliver on an experience, the more likely they are to tell people about it for a shorter period of time at a very high like emotional state. And it's that emotion, the joy in that person, the approval in that eager, excitement, and enthusiasm that builds a great experience.

Jim: I'll give you an example. I went this morning to pick up my taxes from my accountant.

Andrew: Yeah [chuckle].

Jim: I'm getting a refund, which is great. Small businesses like this always ask me, "What can I do as an accountant or a plumber to create a better experience because my business is boring?"

Andrew: Yeah. Well, here's the thing. I think there are three things in here. One, you can raise anticipation for the product or service you're delivering.

So, here's what happens. I don't know about your tax person, but my tax guy is a guy literally. And I send him like a binder of stuff and then I don't want to hear from him for three or four months. And then all of a sudden I get an email with a PDF that I'm supposed to review, right?

Nothing happened in between those times in my mind. And raising anticipation is one of the most powerful ways for any service provider to get you more excited about the outcome of the product or services being delivered, even when it's taxes.

So, imagine this, imagine if you started thinking about exposing his process to me. I call this the Domino's Pizza Tracker strategy. What if he sends me an email and says, "Hey, I got your packet of information today. What a thorough job you did filling out the survey that I send everyone. Thank you so much for doing that. You'll hear from me with any questions I have."

He's immediately taking the world's basically a commodity experience that everybody offers and doing just one thing to increase my enjoyment, my interaction, my interest, my approval of the decision I made to hire this accountant.

So, if somebody asked me within the next two days of getting that email, "Hey man, I have got to get my taxes done. Do you know an accountant?" His name, of course, is top of mind and I can say, "You know what, I do. He's a great guy. He's very communicative and this is what you should sign up with." That's a great start to an experience.

Just quickly, the other two things you can do are maximize the honeymoon phase. So, let me ask this Jim, when you found out you're getting a refund, what was your immediate reaction?

Jim: Joy.

Andrew: Yeah. Did he seem excited about your refund?

Jim: Except for the exclamation point in the email, no.

Andrew: Yeah, exactly. He has to transfer his excitement and enthusiasm for the fact that he has helped you get some money back into an experience that brings and delivers joy in no other way on accountant can.

I don't know how that goes, but let's just think of some fun things. What if he sent you an animated birthday card-type evite that was like, "Guess what, yeah, you're getting $600 back."? All the sudden you think and feel differently about that experience and all he did was send you an ecard, right? That's maximizing the honeymoon phase.

And then the last thing is to inspire the feelings that you had when you got the refund. So, here's what my accountant does. Next year around the same time of the year, he'll send me that package again. It's this boring formal letter that's like, once again, you're going to work with Accounting XYZ. Please fill this out and send it back to us. That's terrible.

What he needs to do is this - "Hey, you know, last year, we were able to get $600 back for you. That was so much fun working on your accounts. I am really excited about doing the same or even better this year."

And then what he is doing is he is inspiring you by reminding you about the feelings you had when you spent money on his service so that you're more likely to 1. sign up again, but 2. feel really good about that decision. Do those make sense?

Jim: Yeah, that makes a lot of sense. I talk a lot about how we're living in a skippable world where everyone wants to skip everything, to fast-forward through the commercials to watch the next episode on Netflix.

Andrew: Yeah.

Jim: So let's talk about attention in 2019 and beyond. You know it and I know it, we're more distracted than ever. How are marketers in business able to get through people multitasking and dealing with mobile and everything being thrown in their face.

Andrew: I really think that people make time for the things that interest them and you're right, things like Netflix and binge watching maintain people's interest because they're really good at understanding how people's minds work - how the psychology works.

And, you know, I learned in the television business the way to earn people's attention is to create what's called the curiosity gap. It's just a gap between what they know and what they want to know.

So, let's go back to your accounting example. If you're an accountant and you want Jim to pay more attention to you and be more excited about talking to you, what you could do is send Jim an email that says, "Hey Jim, I have to talk to you at 1 pm today. I've got some unbelievably exciting news. Can you make it to that phone call?"

Now, if you get that email and you're like, wow, he's got to talk to me today. He's got some unbelievably exciting news. Sure, I'll clear my calendar to talk at 1. In fact, I might even email him back and say, "Oh my gosh, I can talk now. Let's do this. What's so exciting?"

What he is doing is creating a gap in your curiosity and you will think about it. He will maintain your interest all morning until 1 o'clock because he has created a curiosity gap. You can do this with anything. You can do it with emails or with sales proposals. You can do it with the experiences. You can certainly do it with your marketing.

So, if you're going to create a YouTube video, you've got to remember that to maintain people's interest, it doesn't need to be short, it needs to be interesting and full of little curiosity gaps that keep people's attention.

Jim: I say you become Unskippable not by forcing your customer to pay attention, but when you start thinking of ways to make them want to pay attention.

Andrew: Paying attention is a terrible phrase, by the way. It bothers me because people make it sound like it's a transaction - like I can buy your attention, just like you're saying.

I actually believe that great content, great experiences, great people earn our attention overtime. You have to actually really earn the right to own people's attention. And that's much more like a perspective that forces you to think about how am I going to earn this customer, client, prospects, YouTube viewer's attention? What am I going to do to get them involved and interested in what I'm creating?

Jim: I believe we're at a tipping point with funnels and chatbots and automated systems. I think we're in a bubble that's about to burst.

Andrew: Yeah, definitely. I was just shopping for a car and every single car dealer's website, there was a chatbot. I'm just trying to do some basic research at this point. And every dealer has chatbots that are popping up screaming for attention. And to the point where I didn't want to be on their website.

Now, that is the complete opposite of the experience you want to deliver, right? And I think it becomes like we're in a world where we're trying to over-automate the stuff that really matters.

Marketing automation is another great example, right? I get

this idea that it's supposed to, you know, reduce the number of redundant tasks that a marketer does in the form of interactions with customers and clients.

But the irony of it is that I get a lot of automated emails. These are emails that a person would never write [chuckle]. We have to start asking ourselves, are we forcing people to chat about things they would never actually chat about or we wouldn't chat about with them?

Are we forcing emails down people's throats that they don't want and we would never type out? Well then, that's not great marketing and it's not replacing the human touch. It's just more soft.

Jim: The whole concept of companies like Carvana is born from the fact that people don't want to go to the dealership and have to talk to the manager.

Andrew: Exactly. And why are they doing that? Because the experience is so bad. All we have to do is fix the experience and I think you can make a car dealership that is a great experience.

Jim: I think you could. Capital One is redesigning their banking centers.

Andrew: Yes. There's one by my house and I've been to it. It's like a coffee shop/bank/hangout/entrepreneurial space. It's awesome and that is a much better experience.

And I can see myself sitting there if I was an entrepreneur starting up a business, drinking my coffee, doing my work in the morning. If I have a question about getting a business loan, where's the first place I'm going to go? To the counter that's right over there. That's a great experience and I love it.

You can find Andrew Davis's books, speaking info, and some videos for fun at akandrewdavis.com. You can also follow him on Instagram (@andrewdavishere). Check out Andrew's weekly videos on YouTube by searching Loyalty Loop.

ABOUT THE AUTHOR

" "I inspire the uninspired to create a better business, life or career."

Jim F. Kukral is a professional speaker, author, consultant, dad and wanna be pro fisherman.

He delivers insightful and entertaining keynotes and workshops to organizations on attention-getting marketing, creative branding, and understanding how customers think, react, and most importantly, buy.

Please visit www.JimKukral.com to book Jim to speak at your next event. Workshops are also available.

DEDICATION

To my children Hailey Rose & Jayce Ryan. You are both Unskippable to me in every way. Remember to always be kind, generous and happy in your life. I am proud of you both.

ALSO BY JIM F. KUKRAL

Enjoyed this book? If so, you will enjoy these other books from Jim.

Business Around A Lifestyle (Volumes 1 & 2)

Write A F*ing Book Already!

Go Direct!

And More!